Hidden Lighthouse Publishers

The Awakening

A CONSCIOUS SHIFT TO A HIGHER REALM

Vicky Anderson

Hidden Lighthouse Publishers
#55, 8193 West Coast Rd.
Sooke, BC V9Z 1H3
Ph: 250-664-7366

© 2009 Hidden Lighthouse Publishers

All rights reserved. No part of this book may be used or reproduced in any manner whatsoever without written permission except in the case of brief quotation.

Cover design, page design and composition by V. Anderson
Cover image ©Oblong1 Dreamstime.com

Vogel-cut® Crystal
is a registered trademark of Lifestream Associates, LLC

Bach™ and Rescue® Remedy
are registered trademarks of A Nelson and Co Ltd.

Second Edition

ISBN 978-0-9783367-9-0

To my family...

Contents

Acknowledgements iii
Forward vii

Signs of the Times 9

Beyond Newton 17

Sacred Geometries 33

Shift of the Ages 43

Karmic Connections 59

Evolution of our Soul 67

Duality Consciousness 79

The Baptism 91

There is No Spoon 117

The Lightworker 139

Deceptions en Masse 149

The Fall 161

Afterword 177

Acknowledgements

There are so many beings who have helped me bring this work to completion. I thank my system of spiritual guidance, which includes the Angels who have entered my life, and who have and are lovingly guiding it. I thank also New Millennium Essences whose product definitions helped to inspire me.

Grateful acknowledgement also goes to the channelings of Lee Carroll, Steve Rother, Sarah Biermann, Pamela Rose Kribbe, Kevin Ryerson and others, and to the late Levi H. Dowling who diligently transcribed the sacred story of the life of Jesus, and then published it in an inspirational book titled *The Aquarian Gospel of Jesus the Christ*.

When we observe the stars, we see the
blackness of space; when we turn our
attention inward, we see the Light of God...
                                    Shahalah

Forward

In 1963, the Hindu Swami Prabhavananda included an Introduction to his interpretation of the sermon that was preached by Jesus on the Mount of Olives, as recorded in the biblical Gospel of Matthew. I repeat a portion of it here:

> **I have studied the New Testament as I have studied the scriptures of my own religion, Vedanta. Vedanta evolved from the Vedas, the most ancient of Hindu scriptures, and teaches that all religions are true inasmuch as they lead to one and the same goal -- God-realization. My religion therefore accepts and reveres all the great prophets, spiritual teachers, and aspects of the Godhead worshipped in different faiths, considering them to be manifestations of one underlying truth...**
>
> **As a young monk, I dwelt in close association with most of the monastic disciples of Sri Ramakrishna, the founder of the order to which I belong. These holy men lived in the consciousness of God...**
>
> **One of these disciples of Sri Ramakrishna celebrated Christmas every year by offering special worship to Jesus, a custom which has been observed in all the monasteries of the Ramakrishna Order to the present day. On these occasions fruit, bread, and cake are offered in our Hindu way. Often, there is a lecture on Christ; or the story of the Nativity or the Sermon on the Mount is read...**
>
> **Swami Prabhavananda**

Signs of the Times

I was born under the zodiac sign of Aries, which is traditionally identified by an adult Ram. According to the science of Astrology, the secret desire of an Aries is 'to lead the way for others'.

I grew up in a lovely residential district, in a city in Western Canada. My father was a carpenter and bricklayer who, in the late 1950s, built a little home near a river for his growing family. Born of European descent, he was the eldest of ten children. If I was to describe my father in one phrase, it would be 'the ultimate perfectionist'.

My childhood memory of my eldest sister is one of a self-admitted atheist. She believed that people are a product of their environment. I can remember her once telling me that, when babies are born, they are a 'blank canvas'. But she could never understand why her two sons were developing completely different personalities in spite of the fact that she was raising them both in exactly the same manner.

Ayn Rand was one of her favorite writers. As a Russian-born American Philosopher and the author of several popular books, such as *Atlas Shrugged* and *The Fountainhead*, it was Rand who developed the philosophy of Objectivism. Her philosophical theory of knowledge defines how we can translate our perception into valid concepts that identify the facts of our reality. It rejects both faith and feelings as a means of attaining knowledge.

I can recall my other sister, Lynn, having always been a devout Christian. I admire her for her great faith. She is forever reading verses of the Bible and, every Sunday morning, she dutifully heads off to church for services. In contrast to both of my sisters' views on spirituality, my brothers have always held a religious belief system that is more 'middle-of-the-road'.

My own thoughts of God began around the age of fourteen when I came to the realization that mainstream science, in all its wisdom, hasn't discovered how to create a living tree. I grew to hold typical Christian views but I have never believed that God expects us to show our love for Him from inside a steepled building.

The kingdom of God is within you.
Luke 17:21

There is a Mesoamerican civilization, known as the Maya, which exists throughout southern Mexico and northern Central America. According to the Mayans, the age in which we are currently living marks the end of a 500 year long world cycle they call the Trail of Tears. This cycle began with the Spanish Conquest of the Americas in the sixteenth century and culminated in the destruction of several native civilizations. These included the Maya, as well as the Hopi, Laika and Inca tribes.

Signs of the Times

To the Spanish conquistadors and the Catholic Church of Rome, who considered their knowledge to be dangerous, the spiritual wisdom of these American medicine men and women was a threat. So, in the late 1500s, the Church established an Office for the Extirpation of Idolatries, the sole purpose of which was to eradicate traditional religious practices in North and South America. As a result, the native shaman priests went into seclusion.[1] When the cycle of the Trail of Tears came to a completion in the year 1987, a new cycle began, which they call the Harmonic Convergence.

In celebration of the arrival of this new world cycle, there was a gathering of the indigenous tribal elders, which was held at sacred locations all over the world. According to an ancient Mayan prophecy, called the Thirteen Heavens and Nine Hells, it was 'the point at which the counter-spin of history finally comes to a momentary halt and the still imperceptible spin of post-history commences.'[2]

Unbeknownst to me at the time, the beginning of this cycle of Harmonic Convergence set off a chain of events in my life that would drastically affect who I would become. I was twenty-seven years old, married and the mother of a six-year old daughter.

All that we do now must be done in a sacred manner and in celebration. We are the ones who we have been waiting for.
The Hopi Nation of Oraibi, Arizona

Signs of the Times

In the summer of 1989, I presented a skateboard to my daughter as a gift for her eighth birthday. We took it into the parking lot beside our home to test it out. I had never ridden a skateboard so, when it shot out in front of me, I fell -- hard! The fall shattered the bone in a toe on my right foot. When I was taken to the emergency room at our local hospital, I was given a post-operative boot to wear on that foot, the sole of which was a full inch higher than the sole of my shoes.

I limped around on that foot for a week. When my low back began to ache from the difference in height between the boot and the shoe on my other foot, I made an appointment with my local chiropractor. I had experienced a tremendous amount of relief from chiropractic manipulations in the past. But, in spite of numerous chiropractic treatments to this particular injury, inflammation eventually set in and one of my intervertebral discs herniated.

By Christmas, the bone in my foot had mended. But the pain in my back had become excruciating and I was forced to take a leave of absence from the position I had held for eight years in the Quality Assurance department of a mid-sized computer company. Eventually, I stopped seeing my chiropractor altogether and spent most of each day resting on the floor in my living room.

When war broke out in the Persian Gulf, I started attending church with my sister, Lynn, out of fears I was manifesting about my future. She would drive me to services with the passenger seat folded down, while I laid flat on my back looking out at the skies. As this routine continued into the year 1991, I began to doubt that my world would ever be the same again. I was always playing the role of the Doubting Thomas. But, through it all, Lynn would pray.

On the worst day of my entire life, I remember thinking that, if I just leaned hard enough on the car door, maybe it would fling open and I would be lucky enough to fall out into traffic and become the city's next fatality. After services, a man asked me why I seemed so frightened. I told him about my injury and he said, *"I was in a motorcycle accident and had the same problem for many years. One day, I came home and flushed all my pain killers, sedatives and tranquilizers down the toilet. I just knew that God had healed me and that I didn't need them anymore."* None of the church elders had ever seen that man before that day. And they never saw him again. I had met an Angel.

> **My religion consists of a humble admiration of the illimitable superior Spirit who reveals himself in the slight details we are able to perceive with our frail and feeble mind.**
> **Albert Einstein**

By the summer of 1992, the pain in my back was starting to subside and I was beginning to lead a normal life again. One Saturday morning, I saw an advertisement for a carpet remnant sale at Sears Department store. I needed a small carpet for a bedroom in our basement so I drove myself to the sale to take a look at them.

Signs of the Times

The rolls of carpeting were standing upright, resting against the wall of a room at the back of the furniture department. As I was admiring a remnant I thought would serve my needs, something very heavy fell on my head, and then bounced off of me and onto the floor. It was a roll of carpet. A customer had been attempting to maneuver it away from the wall but lost control of it. One-hundred pounds of free-falling fibres had hit me squarely on top of the head.

The next day, I made an appointment with my chiropractor who adjusted a couple of the vertebrae in my neck. But, even with regular adjustments, I soon developed a chronic neck problem. Massage gave me temporary relief, but, within a few months, I noticed the strength in my neck starting to decrease. At that point, I began an active search for a more definitive answer to my problem. In the process, I saw a variety of different doctors and therapists without any success.

Two years later, my strength had deteriorated to a point where I could no longer read to the end of the first page of a newspaper. This was my second wake-up call.

One day, one of the elders at the church prophesied over me. He said, *"There are still trees all around you. But God is going to bring you out into the sunlight."*

Signs of the Times

**Do not fear, for I am with you;
do not be dismayed, for I am your God.
I will strengthen you and help you...**
Isaiah 41:10

In the spring of 1995, I met a medical doctor who specializes in the rehabilitation of orthopedic injuries using advanced muscle work. He was the only person to give me an accurate diagnosis of my neck injury. I learned that the muscles in my neck and upper back had become imbalanced from the blow I had received to the head. More importantly, he explained that I had slowly developed spinal stenosis, a medical condition in which the spinal canal narrows, and then compresses the spinal cord and nerves that feed the rest of the body.

With a specialized program of relaxation massage, trigger point release and manual traction, he soon had me reading an entire newspaper again. By 1998, I had regained all of the muscle strength I had lost and was teaching classes full-time at the Southern Alberta Institute of Technology – a post-secondary technical school that provides technical training and applied education to meet industry's needs.

He later said to me, *"Of all my patients, you have the highest tolerance for pain. You're stronger than you think."* And, through it all, Lynn had prayed.

Signs of the Times

> **That deep emotional conviction of
> the presence of a superior reasoning power,
> which is revealed in the incomprehensible
> universe, forms my idea of God.**
> **Albert Einstein**

In 1999, I saw an opportunity to form a business partnership with the superintendent of a local college, in a venture that would lead me to enter the field of online learning. This took me out of my role in the classroom and into a role as the co-designer of a software application that delivers training to students by way of the Internet.

Shortly thereafter, I booked a few days off work and flew with my daughter to Vancouver, British Columbia, for a short break. We boarded a ferry and sailed over to the largest of the neighboring southern Gulf Islands. After spending the day exploring the island and its little town, I decided then and there that I was going to own a piece of it. So I signed an offer to purchase a two-acre parcel of old-growth forested land that bordered a beautiful wilderness park. I now had a place to camp every year and to dream about the house I hoped to build there. I was officially an 'island girl'...

Beyond Newton

There are seven divine laws that deal with the philosophical, spiritual and material realms of life. They include the laws of Vibration, Rhythm, Polarity, Correspondence, Gender, Mind and Causation.

The divine Law of Vibration states that nothing rests; everything moves; everything vibrates. The lower the vibration, the slower the vibration; the higher the vibration the faster the vibration. Everything we perceive with our senses is actually vibrations, or *frequencies*, that can either be perceived as color or sound. So the color green is also heard as the musical key of E.

The philosophical and scientific basis for this law can be found in Einstein's theory of relativity and in the last few decades of quantum physics. It can also be found in such ancient philosophies as the Vedas, which are the most ancient scriptures of India, as well as in the Gospel according to John, which reads, 'In the beginning was the Word,' the Word implying the vibration of sound.

These vibrating frequencies are measured in cycles per second, or *hertz*. If a frequency is vibrating fast enough, it is emitted as a color of Light. As a result, if a pianist could press a key above the eighty-eight keys that exist on a piano, that key would produce Light. They could create a chord of Light in the same way they can create a chord of sound. And it would be seen as colors of Light because it would be moving at the speed of Light.

> **Everything is a vibration and its effect...**
> **All the physical matters are**
> **composed of vibration.**
> **Dr. Max Planck, PhD**

At the very leading edge of biophysics today, scientists are recognizing that the molecules in our bodies are actually controlled by these frequencies. In 1974, Dr. Colin W.F. McClare, Ph.D, an Oxford University Bio-Physicist, discovered that electro-magnetic frequencies are roughly one-hundred times more efficient in relaying information within a biological system than physical signals, such as hormones, neurotransmitters and other growth factors.[3]

At that time, the world's foremost authority on electro-medicine and electro-chemically induced cellular regeneration was Dr. Robert O. Becker, a Physician who discovered that there is an analog computer type of healing system that exists within the body.[4]

Dr. Becker found that cells are semi-conductors, which function like transistors, to which there is a direct correspondence with the acupuncture meridian system that was mapped out by the Chinese five-thousand years ago. Dr. Becker was twice nominated for the Nobel Prize for his pioneering work, which laid the foundation for the field of bioelectro-magnetics, the study of how electro-magnetic fields interact with and influence biological processes.

**Man possesses a potential for recovery
through the innate intelligence of
the human structure.**
Dr. George Goodheart

Late in 2003, I suddenly began to experience strange neurological symptoms that were quite intense. Accompanying these symptoms were heart palpitations, fatigue and nausea. My perception of my environment became that of a boat rocking in the waves of the sea. It was as though the room was always moving around and around.

Lynn had been listening to a Christian radio station, which sponsored a local naturopathic clinic that specializes in a form of energetic medicine. So, when I saw no improvement in my symptoms over the next several weeks, I made an appointment with Bob, the naturopathic doctor who worked at the clinic.

Bob is certified in Applied Neurology and Energy Medicine and holds an international license in the art of bio-feedback. During my initial consultation with him, he diagnosed me with a severe sensitivity to artificially-generated electro-magnetic frequencies, the dangers of which Dr. Robert Becker warns about in his book *The Body Electric*. Then, he proceeded to begin rebuilding my health with dietary supplements and homeopathic remedies.

My condition was attributed to a combination of the stenosis in my neck, an overbite that often caused my jaw to make a cracking sound when I ate, and the fact that my little house was sitting at the intersection of two major power lines. This third health problem was my third wake-up call.

> **Wake up, O sleeper, rise from the dead,
> and Christ will shine on you.**
> **Ephesians 5:14**

When two frequencies are brought together, the lower will always rise to meet the higher. This is the principle of *resonance*. When a piano is tuned, a tuning fork is struck, and then brought close to the piano string that carries the same musical tone. The string will then raise its vibration and attune itself to the same rate at which the fork is vibrating.

Resonance is the basis for the science of Energy Medicine, which uses it to promote the return of a healthy energetic pattern from the electro-magnetic. Electro-magnetic energy is the equivalent of the Traditional Chinese Medicine concept of *Qi* and the Hindu Ayurvedic concept of *Prana*. It is from the electro-magnetic pattern of energy that health begins. Health then moves to the molecular, the electro-chemical, the physiological, the metabolic and finally to the cellular.

Bob uses Energy Medicine and the principles of resonance to eliminate sensitivities. By this time, I had become sensitive to just about everything, particularly polyester and other synthetics. So he proceeded to explain to me how he uses the principle of resonance to reprogram the brain and central nervous system so the body learns to accept frequencies to which it is sensitive. Vital energy is then restored and new messages are imprinted in the brain. It is this recoding that prevents the body and mind from reacting abnormally to those same frequencies in the future.

The process involved in treating a sensitivity requires the individual to avoid the allergen for a minimum of twenty-four hours after treatment. During one appointment, I tested negatively toward certain plastics. So, when Bob treated me for the frequencies of the specific plastics to which I was sensitive, I was forced to wear gloves the entire day to prevent my skin from touching them. Unfortunately, toilet seats are generally made out of plastic.

Whenever he needed to test me for sensitivities, Bob would use the science of Applied Kinesiology, a diagnostic system that measures the strength of the muscles in response to questions that are 'asked' of the body in order to make determinations about physiology, skeletal trauma, allergies, nutritional imbalances, emotional states and so on.

Over time, I became very intrigued by kinesiology. Bob would demonstrate the sophistication behind this science by simply writing questions down on paper, and then 'muscle testing' for a response to them – a response that always proved to be accurate.

Soon I began to realize that he was accessing an intelligence that is capable of much more than just measuring a bodily response to a frequency. The principle behind Applied Kinesiology extends way beyond chemistry or biology. It is connected to everything around the body. Behind this process there is a superior intelligence.

> **The Counselor, the Holy Spirit,
> whom the Father will send in my name,
> will teach you all things.**
> John 14:26

Although I was still a resident of the big city, I was now single and living alone with my two Dachshunds, in a little hamlet of homes that stood at the foot of a hill overlooking a nature park. The city in which I was living boasts a population of about one million people. So it was no coincidence that the man who would become my second husband moved into a building complex only a few blocks from my little home on the hill.

Ken was born under the zodiac sign of Pisces, the Fish. According to Astrology, when a Piscean is in their purest form, they are 'psychic, visionary and a guiding Light to all who know them'. But the unfortunate thing about being a Pisces is that their symbol depicts one fish straining to pull itself upward, while another fish is frantically pushing itself downward. And it is in this same way that the Pisces lives his life - as both the sinner and the saint.

In contrast to my childhood while growing up in Happy Swell Meadows, Ken started heading down Damnation Alley at a very young age. His father was an alcoholic who had abandoned him by the time he was five years old.

Three years later, his mother was the victim of a life-threatening accident, which hospitalized her for almost two years, leaving Ken and his two teenaged sisters to run the household on their own.

Free to do as he pleased, Ken soon started smoking, drinking and experimenting with street drugs. His drugs gave him a false sense of security, one that quickly developed into a delusion of grandeur - a condition the Greeks call *megalomania*.

When his high school teacher ordered him to remove the hat he was wearing in class, Ken walked out of the building and never returned. It was his first day in high school and it was also his last. He was fifteen years old and selling drugs for a living.

The late Astrologer, who was known only by the pseudonym Athena Starwoman, once described the Pisces as follows: 'Some can be found leading the field in many diverse areas of life and many are represented among successful millionaires. Others, however, often find themselves living in a reform school or another type of institution. Because of their inner world of fantasy, Pisces people seldom perceive whatever is going on around them in its true Light. They perceive life as they want to perceive it, coloring their view of the world in hues and tones that are far removed from its true reflection.'

Beyond Newton

> **We all start from naive realism,
> i.e., the doctrine that
> things are what they seem.**
> **Bertrand Russell**

At the age of twenty-six, Ken met the woman with whom he began his third serious relationship. One evening, she suddenly changed her mind about the plans they had made for their New Years celebration, and then left the house without him. Ken later found her at a friend's house, in bed with his business partner. When Ken moved out of their home, his partner moved in.

According to Astrology, the life pursuit of a Pisces is 'to avoid feeling alone'. As a result, one thing that wreaks havoc in their lives is romance. When things are going well for them romantically, they live on 'cloud nine'. But, when that romance turns sour, they land face down in a heap.

Ken was now living out of the back of his van. He was never without a drink in his hand and often fell asleep that way. The Piscean syndrome can lead people into some of the most unusual and unlikely living conditions. Of all the signs of the zodiac, it is the Pisces who ends up in the most predicaments.

On September 1, 2001, Ken checked himself into a recovery center for alcoholics. While two American jetliners were being flown into the World Trade Center, Ken was adjusting to life in a recovery house that was sponsored by Alcoholics Anonymous - a fellowship of people who share their experience, strength and hope in an effort to solve their alcoholism.

The Alcoholics Anonymous, or AA, program provides for the basic needs of its 'disciples' because, at the time in their lives when they become members, they cannot deal with even the very smallest of life's responsibilities. The program is self-supporting through the contributions of its members and there are no fees or dues. The only requirement for membership is a sincere desire to stop drinking.

By simply starting on this path for their own sake, a member automatically completes the first step of the AA program, which requires them to 'admit that they are powerless over alcohol'. If they are then asked if they believe that a power greater than themselves can restore their sanity, most members say, "Certainly!" This is the second step in the program. But the third and most important step requires them to actually turn their lives over to the care of that 'higher power'. This, then, begins the slow process of the breaking down of the ego.

Find God.
That is the only purpose in Life.
Sri Ramakrishna

One day, a sponsor of the AA program loaned Ken a book titled *The Sermon on the Mount According to Vedanta*. It was written by the Hindu Swami Prabhavananda. This swami is an early-twentieth century teacher of the Vedanta philosophy, a philosophy that follows the Vedas. The basic teachings of the Vedantas are that there is a oneness to all life; that God exists in all beings; that our real nature is divine.

> **I came into the world,**
> **to testify to the truth.**
> **John 18:37**

Most alcoholics are either atheists or agnostics. And Ken was no exception. But he read Prabhavananda's little book, and then made a list of all the people whom he had wronged and of those who had wronged him. He took his list of wrong-doings to the top of a mountain and, in the presence of a church pastor, he read it aloud. He then burned each piece of paper and asked that God remove each of his shortcomings. This process was Ken's baptism and it fulfilled steps five and six of the AA program.

> **If you really wish to alter your life...**
> **then Jesus, in his Sermon on the**
> **Mount of Olives, has clearly shown you**
> **how it is to be done.**
> **Emmet Fox**

It was the summer of 2004 when Ken and I first met. He immediately proceeded to tell me that he was a recovered alcoholic. I admired him for his honesty and it was apparent that we were destined to become soul mates. Four months later, we were engaged to be married.

Aries people love challenges. In fact, if everything is running smoothly, we are quite capable of deliberately 'rocking the boat'. And that is just what I did. I sold my little home on the hill and my 'island getaway' and then moved with Ken into a big house on Mayne Island, one of the smallest of the islands on the West Coast.

Over time, I began to focus more and more on a balanced, holistic lifestyle and was influenced to replace all chemical cleansers with biodegradables, such as vinegar and water. I started reading all the labels on food jars and packages. I became acutely aware of anything that was not natural and organic, and I was very adamant about ingesting natural things and of having only natural things around me.

Bob had eliminated the majority of the sensitivities I had developed before we moved to the West Coast. But I was still very intolerant of artificially-generated frequencies, like those produced by computers, television sets and other electronics. As a result, I had to be very aware of my surroundings at all times. Electro-magnetic energy cannot be seen so it was a hard 'game' to play.

During the first two years of island life, my five physical senses became very sensitive to extremes. I grew increasingly intolerant of loud noises, strong chemical smells, and so on. Eventually, I developed a severe case of insomnia, during which I would lie awake staring at the backs of my eyelids for most of the night and, on some nights, getting no sleep at all.

I began to study everything I could about the physiology of the human body. While my daughter was studying this type of material in a classroom at a major university, I was learning it first-hand. Eventually, I learned that the nerves at the back of my head were blocked and energy was not capable of moving smoothly through them.

**The only source of knowledge
is experience.**
Albert Einstein

Ken wanted me to turn my life over to my higher power in the same way he had. But Aries are fire signs and those born under the fire element are regarded as being assertive and independent. So instead, I continued to play 'telephone therapy' with Bob even though Ken would calmly say to me, *"Let go of the steering wheel."* Where the element of Aries is fire, the element of Pisces is water. Whenever my fire would start to run too hot, Ken would gently put it out.

**The stone the builders rejected
has become the cornerstone.**
Matthew 21:42

In my research into Energy Medicine, I learned that, during World War I, an Englishman named Dr. Edward Bach was a practicing Physician in London. After the war, he became a homeopathic practitioner and completed a large amount of research in the field of homeopathy.[5]

As a Pathologist and Bacteriologist, Dr. Bach was able to develop vaccines from intestinal bacteria. He discovered that doses are most beneficial if they are repeated only when improvement resulting from the previous dose has ceased. As a homeopath, he expanded this work to develop remedies that he could administer orally, rather than by injection. These are still known today as the Bach Nosodes.[6]

In the year 1930, Dr. Bach gave up his lucrative medical practice in London to devote the rest of his life to finding what he believed to be a system of Energy Medicine. He soon discovered that, like the plant from which they spring forth, flowers have a vibrational component. Because the flower is a plant's crowning achievement, its essence carries its highest frequency.[7]

Dr. Bach's research eventually led him to develop a process with which he could extract the electro-magnetic pattern of a flower while it was in bloom. Unlike homeopathy, which works directly on the physical body, he learned that these electro-magnetic frequency patterns work on human consciousness.

After some research into the effectiveness of flower essences on humans today, I learned that veterinarians worldwide also use Dr. Bach's flower essences in the treatment of animals. Their use is in the treatment of emotional problems, such as the fear of loud noises, excessive barking or hissing, shock, trauma or mistreatment, a loss of a companion, separation anxiety or adapting to new surroundings. This natural form of healing is one of the more evolved systems of rehabilitation. And it uses nothing but energy in a preserved form.

> **Five hundred years before Christ some physicians of ancient India... advanced the art of healing to so perfect a state that they were able to abolish surgery.**
> Dr. Edward Bach, MD

Around that time, I decided to try a popular combination of Bach™ essences, which is made from five different flowers. This powerful group of essences, called Rescue® Remedy, is fused together to provide a popular treatment for the specific imbalances that are caused by stress. Within a few days, an overwhelming sensation of calmness suddenly came over me. This was a sensation I had never felt before. It was like the hand of God had lifted me up onto a cloud, from which I was looking down on my world of problems.

I knew there was an enormous amount of power in these essences and I felt compelled to find out how to leverage it. Through a book, titled *Flower Essences and Vibrational Healing*, I learned that the difference between the manifestations of the physical, mental, emotional and spiritual result simply from varying frequencies. So, when taken regularly, flower essences enhance our concept of ourselves as beings of energy. They provide for one of the most evolved systems of healing on the planet and activate ancient doorways to levels of consciousness that have long since been forgotten.

Beyond Newton

When the essence of a flower is ingested, it settles midway between the circulatory and nervous systems, where an electro-magnetic current is then established by the polarity of these two systems. Our consciousness uses these properties to stimulate our physical body.

To actually see the physical healing property of these essences, we can place bacteria into two cultures, and then add to one of them a drop of the essence from a flower with a very high frequency, such as the Lotus. If both cultures are frozen for the same amount of time and are then allowed to thaw, the untreated culture will show little or no signs of life, whereas the treated culture will be very much alive. These intrinsic vibrational patterns exist at the atomic level in all matter.

All life is simply different levels of vibrating energy. This is Einstein's famous $e=mc^2$ equation in which energy is related to matter and to the speed of Light squared.

Although the frequencies of a flower essence provide for a 'one size fits all' vibration, as long as its frequency is close to that which is required, a person will resonate with it. And the higher our frequencies are raised, the higher our consciousness is raised. The higher our consciousness is raised, the purer our mind, body and spirit becomes.

I will raise him up at the last day.
                                                          I John 6:40

One of the essences I learned about is made from the flower of the plant of the White Yarrow. This essence offers protection from radiation. The shape of its flowers disrupts radiation waves because radiation travels at the same angles and is dispersed when it meets a similar field. Because I was still extremely sensitive to artificially-generated frequencies, I started regularly ingesting the White Yarrow flower essence. After four months, I began to notice an improvement in my overall condition.

One morning, I felt so strong I decided to skip my morning dose of the White Yarrow essence that I had made a part of my daily routine. But, within just a few hours, I started feeling very hot and feverish, my heart started to pound and electric shocks began to surge through my left hand. By missing that dose, I had thrown my electro-magnetics into shock. My consciousness had been resonating with the protective Light of the essence. And, when I 'turned out the light,' my body had run straight into a wall...

Sacred Geometries

By this time, the concept of frequencies and resonance had become a topic of extreme importance to me. I learned that there are formats of frequency and resonance in the construction of the Great Pyramid of Giza in Egypt, which relate both to nature and to natural events. These formats are mathematically perfect sets.

There are five geometric shapes, which have faces, edges and angles that are congruent. Named after the Greek philosopher, Plato, each of these *Platonic Solids* produces specific energetic effects. The pyramid is one of these shapes. In geometry, it is known as the Tetrahedron.

The energetic power of the geometric shape of the pyramid is that it creates a force field that preserves everything under it in a state of perfection. The word *pyramid* takes its origins from the Greek meaning 'fire in the center of'.

When two opposing pyramids are merged, they create a Star of David, which is the symbol of Judaism - a set of religious beliefs and practices that originated from the Hebrew Bible. In geometry, the Star of David is known as the Star Tetrahedron. It is interesting to note that, when written on top of each other, the letters in the ancient language of Hebrew together form the Star Tetrahedron.

Sacred Geometries

**Magic is what we call any science
we do not understand.**
Arthur C. Clarke

In the early 1980's, Dr. Robert J. Gilbert, Ph.D, was an instructor in the U.S. Marine Corps, in the field of nuclear, biological and chemical warfare survival. During that time, he became aware of a thriving sub-culture of advanced scientists who are studying geometric shapes as a key to everything from Human Biology to Nuclear Physics. This includes studies that have been commissioned by NATO.[8]

Dr. Gilbert found that, in experiments in Nano-technology, the study of the control of matter at an atomic and molecular scale, scientists were unsuccessful in their attempts to create matter until they studied sacred geometric shapes, such as the pyramid.

Where there is matter, there is geometry.
Johannes Kepler

In 1959, a Czechoslovakian radio engineer, named Karl Drbal, received a patent for a model pyramid that regenerates a dull steel razor blade to its full sharpness. His patented method of sharpening a blade involves pointing one angle of the pyramid toward true north, and then placing the blade under the pyramid so the edge lies in the direction of the Earth's electro-magnetic gridlines. The magnetic energy of the Earth then sharpens the blade by steadily decreasing the number of disturbances in the bonds of its structure.[9]

Sacred Geometries

One of the originators of the concept of wormholes was Dr. Wesley H. Bateman. In 1975, Dr. Bateman, who held a Ph.D. in mathematics, began studying the measurements of the Great Pyramid. His work spanned a total of thirty-two years, during which he discovered the sophisticated mathematical system that was used by the original architects when they defined the measurements of the shape of this ancient structure. He also learned that the same mathematical system was used to define the ancient Mayan Pyramid of the Sun in southern Mexico.[10]

The accuracy of the workmanship that went into the construction of the Great Pyramid is such that the four sides of its massive 5.3 sq. km. base are only one minute in angle off of a perfect square. There are at least nine mathematical formats in its measurements, each of which has its own version of all the known mathematical constants, including *pi* and *phi*. Denoted by letters of the Greek alphabet, *pi* and *phi* are the most universal principals found in nature. *Phi* is well-known to exist at the end of a series of numbers, called the Fibonacci, in which each number is the sum of the previous two.

Dr. Bateman has found that the system, which was used to measure the Great Pyramid, is the same mathematical system that God built into all of Creation. It is sacred geometry - a complex system of symbols and structures involving Space and Time. All of nature and biology are highly organized systems, which generate fractal structures that obey the *phi* ratio.

Sacred Geometries

**Moses was educated in all the
Wisdom of the Egyptians.**
Acts 7:22

These same mathematical ratios are also found in sacred art. It has recently been discovered that there are several pieces of sacred art of the Renaissance and Baroque periods that call attention to the index finger of St. John the Baptist, which clearly points away from the rest of his fingers at 23.5 degrees - the exact mathematical angle at which the Earth spins in relation to the Sun.

This geometric symbolism can be seen in numerous works by many famous painters of that period, including Leonardo Da Vinci, François Le Moyne, Jusepe de Ribera, Titian, Mathis Gothart, Jean Clouet, Raphael, El Greco, Caravaggio, Valentin de Boulogne, Nicolas Regnier, Caravaggio, Paolo Veronese, Bacaccio and Bartolomé Esteban Murillo. But this curious oddity has gone unnoticed for hundreds of years.[11]

The mathematical ratios found in nature are also found in music. Dr. Paolo deBernadis, Ph.D, is Professor of Physics at the University La Sapienza in Rome and a former member of the Astronomy Working Group of the European Space Agency. His fields of expertise include Experimental Astrophysics and Cosmology. In 2001, he led a team of researchers in an experiment involving an extremely sensitive microwave telescope that allowed them to probe backwards through Space and Time to the Big Bang.[12]

Sacred Geometries

> **The early Universe is full of sound waves compressing and rarefying matter and light, much like sound waves compress and rarefy air inside a flute or trumpet.**
>
> Dr. Paolo deBernadis, PhD

The intense radiation that filled the Universe when it was first created is still detectable as a faint glow. So the stars, planets and other structures that were present at that time left their imprint in the background radiation. The details of the harmonics that exist there have allowed Dr. deBernadis and his team to understand the nature of the Universe.

The variations in the background radiation are as fine as 100-millionth of one degree in temperature. By measuring these subtle variations, Dr. deBernadis and his researchers have uncovered a harmonic sequence of reverberations they call the Music of Creation.

> **Using a music analogy, last year we could tell what note we were seeing – if it was C sharp or F flat. Now, we can tell not only which note is being played, but also what instrument is playing it.**
>
> Dr. Barth Netterfield

One-hundred years ago, the international music industry changed from what was the Pythagorean method of tuning musical instruments to what is now an equal temperament method. When using this new tuning method, only the octaves are pure; the notes in between are now tempered. As a result, every semi-tone has the same mathematical ratio.[13]

Just like artificially-generated electro-magnetic frequencies are impure, so are the frequencies that are generated by all musical instruments that have been manufactured since the turn of the twentieth century. So the musical compositions and recordings they have produced don't match the frequencies God built into nature and into our physical bodies.

In 1974, a Naturopath named Dr. Joseph S. Puleo, N.D., discovered an ancient hymn to St. John the Baptist called *Hymnus in Ioannem*. This hymn is sung, 'So that your servants may freely sing forth the wonders of your deeds, remove all stain of guilt from their unclean lips, O Saint John.' It was written by an eighth century Lombard historian and was then given to the Roman Catholic Church.[14]

This hymn contains a musical scale, called the Solfeggio, which includes the six tones Ut, Re, Mi, Fa, Sol and La. The tone of Ut takes its origins from the Latin term *UT-queant laxis*, which means 'the whole series of recognized musical notes'. This tone vibrates at a frequency of 396 Hz. When we resonate with this frequency, it helps to shift our consciousness away from fear and guilt, which prepares our hearts to receive the other tones in the scale.

The tone of Mi originates from the Latin term *MI-ra gestorum* meaning 'miracle'. When tuned using the new tuning method, this tone vibrates at a frequency of 512 Hz. But when tuned using the original method of tuning, this same tone has a frequency of 528 Hz, which is used for transformation and miracles. It is also the frequency used by genetic biochemists to repair damaged human DNA.

The tone of Re originates from *RE-sonare fibris*, meaning 'resonance'. Vibrating at a frequency of 417 Hz, it is for facilitating change through resonance. The frequency of the tone of Fa is 639 Hz, which is for connecting and relationships, the 741 Hz tone of Sol is for solutions and expressions, and the 852 Hz tone of La is for the awakening of our intuition and the expansion of our consciousness.

> **The number from the tribe of Judah was 74,600.**
> **Numbers 1:27**

The first five books of the Hebrew Bible are known collectively as the Torah. There exists an ancient set of interpretations, called *Bamidbar Rabbah*, which is holy to Judaism. One of these interpretations states that there are seventy layers of meaning encrypted within the Torah.

One of the books of the Torah is the *Book of Numbers*. In chapter seven, verses 12 through 83 of this book, there is a pattern of six repeating codes. When deciphered using the Pythagorean method of reducing numbers to their single digit integers, the codes in those verses reveal the six frequencies in the original Solfeggio scale of musical tones.

> The one who brought his offering on
> the First day was of the tribe of Judah.
> **Numbers 7:12**

The language of ancient Hebrew is a highly unusual language. In 1977, a Harvard University trained teacher of Hebrew, named Uri Harel, began to explore and dissect this language. As a Biblical scholar, he believed that one of the seventy layers of meaning in the Torah is music. As a result, he dedicated years of research to tapping on a musical keyboard in an effort to find a formula that would unlock the musical patterns he believed are encrypted in these original Hebrew texts.[15]

> I was able to come up with a formula,
> so to speak, to be able to take a
> Hebrew letter and to find its frequency
> translated into a musical note.
> **Uri Harel**

Harel was able to assign a specific frequency to each of the letters in the Hebrew alphabet. When he assigned these frequencies to each of the letters that make up the words in eight of the books of *Psalms* in the Hebrew Bible, as well as to parts of the biblical *Book of Exodus*, which is part of the Torah, he discovered beautiful classically-arranged compositions.

> We have opened the way for a new kind
> of Bible translation – not into yet
> another spoken language, but into the
> Universal language of music.
> **Uri Harel**

With the help of a well-known composer, violinist and guitarist, Harel has recorded the beautiful music he has found to exist in the books of the Hebrew Bible. But, what is most interesting is that, when the books are translated from Hebrew into any other language, the information, knowledge and understanding of these texts is diminished to such an extent that it becomes impossible to duplicate the musical effect...

Sacred Geometries

Shift of the Ages

Mayne is a relaxed island. At only 23 sq km, it is the tiniest of the southern Gulf Islands. Idyllic meadows and wildflowers are its most distinguishing characteristics. But the history behind the landmarks gives it its unique charm. So, shortly after we left the big city and moved to Mayne Island, I had written an historical book about the pioneers who forged its frontier in the mid-1800s.

By the spring of 2008, I had researched and written eight historical books about the Gulf Islands. I loved to write about the pioneers. They showed me a simpler time when the land was unspoiled, when children helped with the family business and where there was honor in that business. Most of these people immigrated to the islands from England, Ireland and Scotland. I made it my passion to piece together their histories.

One afternoon, while doing some historical research, I accidentally stumbled onto a book that spoke of a theory of the world coming to an end around the year 2012. The author of the book claimed to have proven his theory using quantum physics, a set of principles underlying the most fundamental description of all physical systems, the most notable of which is the prediction of probabilities in situations where typical physics predicts certainties.

When I told Ken about what I had read, he chuckled and said, *"Oh, Hun - I'm not going to change my life just because someone wrote a book about how the world is coming to an end."* In spite of Ken's apparent lack of interest in the matter, I felt compelled to find out just what was behind this theory.

> **To those who listen to my teaching,
> more understanding will be given, and they
> will have an abundance of knowledge.**
> **Matthew 13:12**

In the early 1970s, a Philosopher named Terence McKenna used an ancient Chinese text, called the *I Ching*, as the basis for a complex mathematical formula, which calculates the ebb and flow of dynamic change in the Universe as an inherent quality of Time. Also known as the *Book of Changes*, the *I Ching* contains a series of sixty-four binary hexagrams that are used to identify order in random events.[16]

This ancient book describes a sophisticated system of cosmology and philosophy that is intrinsic to ancient Chinese cultural beliefs. It centers on the dynamic balance of opposites, the evolution of events and the acceptance of the inevitability of change.

In McKenna's mathematical formula, when dynamic change is graphed over Time, a fractal waveform known as the Timewave results. His Timewave calculator predicts the specific periods in history in which the dynamics of change either increase or decrease.

After a nuclear physicist revised his formula, McKenna's calculator was then written in Java and released to the public as *Timewave One*. The graph it produces predicts waves of dynamic change that suddenly cease during the winter of the year 2012.

> **There will be signs in the
> Sun, Moon and Stars.**
> **Luke 21:25**

Astrology is the oldest science on Earth. It is driven by gravity and magnetics, which are the forces that shift the position of the planets around the Sun. Translated from the Greek *zoidiakos kyklos*, which means 'circle of animals,' the astrological zodiac of constellations encircles the sky on each side of the path in which the Earth orbits the Sun.

At this precise period in history, both the Sun and the Earth are moving into a perfect line with the center of our galaxy, in an exquisite galactic alignment called the Holy Cross. This alignment occurs only once in every 26,000 years. The ancient Egyptian cultures understood that it takes that long for the Earth to pass through one complete cycle of the twelve constellations of the zodiac. The Maya, Hopi, Laika and Inca also know this.

In Hindu philosophy, this 26,000 year cycle involves the process of falling asleep and awakening, behind which is an ongoing evolution of consciousness. They break the cycle into *yugas*, which they call the Kali, Dvapara, Treta and Saatya yugas.

Shift of the Ages

The ancient Greeks broke this same great cycle of sleeping and awakening into ages they called the Iron, Bronze, Silver and Golden ages. Modern astrologers calculate it as a cycle that involves the gradual change in the orientation of the Earth's axis of rotation. They refer to it as the Precession of the Equinoxes.

> **Then those also who have
> fallen Asleep in Christ are lost.**
> I Corinthians 15:18

The ancient Maya were a culture that studied the long cycles of vibration on the Earth. To do this, they developed a very sophisticated calendar called the Tzolk'in, which is based on a 13:20 mathematical ratio. This calendar isn't the oldest known calendar in existence. But it is the most accurate. Where our own calendar year results in an error of 3.02 days over the course of 10,000 years, the calculation of the Mayan Tzolk'in calendar year results in an error of only 1.98 days over that same number of years.[17]

The Mayans were consummated astronomers who used their calendar to prophesy that this current period in history is a major shift of the ages. They prophesy that, from out of this galactic alignment, 'the god Quetzalcoatl will return to Earth by way of a serpent rope'.

The prophecies of the Maya, Hopi, Laika and Inca all say that humanity is currently in the process of a very rapid evolutionary jump. They foretell that the end of this 26,000 year cycle is the beginning of an age of evolution – that we are at a turning point in human history, a period in which a new species of human will soon give birth to itself.

> **There before me was a great multitude that
> no one could count, from every nation, tribe,
> people and language, standing before the
> throne and in front of the Lamb.**
> **Revelation 7:9**

The divine Law of Rhythm states that everything flows out and in; everything has its tides; all things rise and fall; the pendulum-swing manifests in everything; the measure of the swing to the right is the measure of the swing to the left; rhythm compensates.

There is a to-and-fro, ebb-and-flow and up-and-down swing to everything in life. The 24 hour cycle of day and night, the 365 day cycle of the seasons and the 26,000 year precession of the equinoxes are all caused by the Earth spinning on its polar axis of 23.5 degrees in relation to the Sun.

> **There is a Time for everything, and a
> season for every activity under Heaven...
> a Time to be born and a Time to die...
> a Time to tear down and a Time to build.**
> **Ecclesiastes 3:1-3**

Like the transition from night to day and from winter to summer, both of which move us through darkness and into Light, one complete 26,000 year cycle transitions us through the dark ages and into ages of spiritual enlightenment. And, on our calendar, this continuous cycle comes to a completion during the winter of the year 2012.

> **What has been will be again,**
> **what has been done will be done again;**
> **there is nothing new under the Sun.**
> **Ecclesiastes 1:9**

There are models that attempt to explain the spin of the Earth. But the origin of the energy behind that spin was unknown until two physicists, named Drs. Nassim Haramein and Elizabeth Rauscher, Ph.D., recently amended Einstein's equations that describe gravity. Their amendment accounts for a fundamental force in Space-Time generating torque. This torque forces the Space-Time 'manifold' to spin in the same way the engine of a car applies torque to the wheels in order for them to rotate. And it originates from a change in the density of the geometry of Space and Time.[18]

When we measure a solid geometric shape, its width, length and height determine its Spatial dimensions. So everything in the physical third dimension can be described mathematically using three numbers. But, there is a fourth dimension - Time.

Dr. Haramein arrived at many of his conclusions by observing sacred geometry and mathematical ratios, and from ancient symbols and Hebrew and Egyptian texts. Dr. Haramein is the Director of The Resonance Project, a non-profit organization dedicated to the unification of science and philosophy. His partner, Dr. Rauscher, is a renowned Astro-physicist and Nuclear Scientist who was Professor of Physics at John F. Kennedy University of California. She is currently a consultant to the NASA Space Shuttle Program.

> **Find the fundamental forces necessary to
> generate spin since, if those were known,
> we would ultimately know
> the foundations of Reality.**
> Dr. Nassim Haramein

Gregg Braden is an Engineer and Geologist who has become a leading authority on synthesizing science with spiritual teachings from around the world. In his book, *Awakening to Zero Point*, he writes about how the spin of the Earth is slowing down and its frequency is increasing.

The Earth has a frequency that is known as the Schumann Resonance. This frequency has held constant at around 7.83 Hz per second since at least the turn of the last century when it was first measured. The military based its global communications on this frequency because it was considered to be constant.[19]

In 1987, the year the indigenous tribal elders gathered to celebrate the cycle of the Harmonic Convergence, the Earth's frequency suddenly began to increase. By the dawn of this new millennium, the resonant frequency of the Earth had risen to around 9 Hz. The word *harmonic* is defined as 'a signal whose frequency is an integral multiple of the frequency of a reference signal.' The word *convergence* denotes 'the approach toward a fixed state'.

As the frequency of the Earth has been increasing, so has our concept of Time. The National Institute of Standards and Technology, which assists the entire world in maintaining a uniform system of Time, has recently been making unexpected adjustments to their atomic clocks to compensate for this sudden increase in Time.

Dr. Lyn Hopkins, Ph.D., is the director of a center for the study and practice of esoteric healing and psychology. She believes that Time is the mathematics for the universal laws of nature. The Mayans knew this. The frequency of Time is the 13:20 ratio on which their Tzolk'in calendar is based. The proportions of this mathematical ratio are the basis for all sacred geometry. It is Time that keeps order in our universe. And, in this age, Time is breaking up.

> **We speak of God's secret wisdom,**
> **a wisdom that has been hidden**
> **and that God destined for our glory**
> **before Time began.**
> **Corinthians 2:6-8**

For decades, physicists have puzzled over the weakness of the force of gravity in comparison to the other fundamental forces of nature. A tiny magnet can lift a paper clip, even though all the mass of the Earth is pulling it in the opposite direction.

Einstein was unsuccessful in coming up with a unified theory that could apply equally well to gravity and all the other forces. But, in 1967, a decade after he died, his successors began to focus on a new theory – one that involves 'strings'.

String theory is a developing branch of theoretical physics that combines quantum mechanics and general relativity into a theory of gravity. It is the first theory to describe the natural forces of gravity, matter, electro-magnetics, and weak and strong interactions, all in a mathematically complete system.

Some physicists believe this theory is the correct fundamental description of nature – that the building blocks of the Universe are not sub-atomic particles, but rather, they are a more fundamental layer of infinitesimally small filaments of vibrating energy. And these strings of energy vibrate at different frequencies.

> **I don't think it's ever happened that a theory that has the kind of mathematical appeal that String theory has turned out to be entirely wrong.**
> **Dr. Steven Weinberg, PhD**

The mathematics involved in String theory point to the existence of other dimensions that are beyond our familiar world. According to this theory, we are living in a universe that has eleven dimensions, with parallel dimensions, such as sub-space and hyper-space, which exist alongside it. Our universe is actually part of a 'multiverse' of events that exist simultaneously in various Time frames. It obscures a reality that is far richer and more complex than anyone ever imagined.

A standard analogy is to consider multi-dimensional space as a garden hose. If the hose is viewed from a sufficient distance, it appears to have only one dimension - length. If we move closer to the hose, we see that it also has other dimensions - width and height. So we can see that the hose has at least three dimensions. If an ant crawled into the opening of that hose, it would be able to move in two dimensions inside it. And, if a bee flew into the opening, it would be able to move in three dimensions inside it.

But these extra dimensions are only visible at an extremely close range, or by experimenting with particles that have extremely small wavelengths that, in quantum mechanics, means very high frequencies.

> **How Wide and Long and High and Deep
> is the Love of Christ.**
> I Ephesians 3:18

At this point in my quest, I started asking God to show me the whole truth of my existence. It would be an understatement to say that, almost immediately, I was given broader, more enlightened perspectives on reality.

> **For everyone who asks receives;
> he who seeks finds; and to him who
> knocks, the door will be opened.**
> Matthew 7:7-8

God revealed to me that dimensions are realms of consciousness that abide by certain energetic laws. In physics, the dimensions of a system are referred to as its 'degrees of freedom'. Three-dimensional objects don't have a lot of freedom. They move slowly so they are perceived as being solid. But, the fact of the matter is - there is no matter.

At higher dimensional levels, energies are less dense because their vibration is much quicker. Subsequently, anything that exists in those energy fields is moving too fast for our senses to be able to detect them. And it requires a lot of energy for them to lower their vibration to a point where they can be perceived in our reality.

> **There is no place in this new kind of physics both for the Field and Matter, for the Field is the only Reality.**
> **Albert Einstein**

By this time, Ken and I had moved to Vancouver Island - the big island. So I began looking for a naturopath who had established a practice there, one who was working with Energy Medicine and the science of Applied Kinesiology. Within a few days, I was led to meet Don, a naturopathic physician who was born with autism - a condition characterized by repetitive behavior.

Autism is considered by modern science to be a brain development disorder. But what science does not yet understand is that the autistic person can perceive in multiple dimensions. They have non-linear minds. As a result, the autistic person will spend a lifetime trying to overcome the frustrations of linear thought - thought that has a beginning and an end. The only energies that calm them are those that are multi-dimensional, such as the colors in art and the sounds in music.

With musical compositions, there is no limit to the number of sounds that can be heard and assembled simultaneously; the more that are added, the more beautiful the music becomes. And there is no limit to the number of colors that can be comprehended and resolved in a pattern; the more that are added, the more spectacular is the design.

> **The most beautiful thing we can experience is the Mysterious. It is the source of all true Art and Science.**
> **Albert Einstein**

During one of my initial appointments with Don, he said to me, *"You have a lot of power. You don't know it yet because it's being channeled."* As I laid on his examining table, I saw him look up toward the wall, nod, and then ask, *"Do you want me to treat her heart too?"* At that moment, I realized that he was actually receiving messages. In fact, he seemed to confer regularly with entities from another realm, which he could both see and hear.

> **Your sons and your daughters shall prophesy, your old men shall dream dreams, your young men shall see visions.**
> **Joel 2:28-29**

Dr. Sonia Choquette, Ph.D, is a world-renowned author and spiritual teacher who holds a BA, MS and Ph.D in Metaphysics and is highly trained in Metaphysical Law. In her book, *Ask Your Guides*, she writes that everyone has a spiritual support system, which dispenses understanding to us of both a spiritual and a philosophical nature.

Our spiritual 'guides' work indirectly by placing us in the right place at the right time, or by leading us to find the right people who can help to expand our awareness so we can fully embrace our potential as divine beings. The main goal of our guides is to help us understand who we really are. And they will use every means possible to attract our attention, including communicating telepathically and through the dream, or astral, state.

Our world of perception has many dimensions. But most of them are inaccessible to us because we have been trained to focus on only a small bandwidth of experiences. Until we experience these dimensions, they don't exist for us because they are outside our range of perception. So, in order to experience them, we must alter our brain activity.

The mind is more powerful than any particle accelerator, more sensitive than any radio receiver or the largest optic.
Terence Mckenna

Modern science has labeled the cerebrum of our brain 'the sleeping giant'. But the cerebrum is actually the centre of electro-magnetic resonating power. It is through this centre that all spiritual awareness occurs.

The pineal gland is our positive contact point. It acts as a neuro-endocrine transducer, which transmits information as signals that direct the pituitary gland by way of the hypothalamus gland. As the master control center in the brain, the pituitary gland is our negative contact point. It acts as a receiver, which enables information to be placed in the cerebrum of our brain.[20]

The cerebral cortex gathers information for our various levels of communication. Within it are pyramidal cells that are the primary excitation unit of the pre-frontal cortex. Because of their ability to convert electro-magnetic frequencies into electrical currents, these cells function as liquid Crystals. As a result, if we 'still' the cerebral cortex, we can use telepathy to connect with entities in higher dimensions of consciousness.

> **Ayn Rand's intellectual genius was great, but far greater still was her willingness to tune in to her Spirit, feel her Spirit, live by her Spirit, and write from her Spirit.**
>
> **Brian Eenigenburg**

In our small West Coast town is a used bookstore, called The Reading Room, which sports a beautiful bronze Angel on its storefront. One Saturday, while I was browsing the few titles in the spiritual and religious sections of the store, I was led to find the book *The Sermon on the Mount*. When he saw it in my hand, Ken said, *"That's the exact same book I was given to read when I was in the AA program!"*

As I read the little book, I realized that, if I listen for that 'still small voice,' God would always send me a messenger to lead me straight to what I needed to know, every moment of every day. If we keep our hearts and minds focused on Him, and ask only Him to show us the truth, only He can and will answer. The things that will then be bestowed upon us are illumination and joy, unconditional love, peace of mind, self-awareness, fearlessness and forgiveness. These are the fruits of God's grace.

People often wonder why their lives are so challenging. Sometimes, our doors are shut as a deliberate attempt by our spiritual guidance system to get us to focus our attention on God. You don't have to go very far to hear this story. Many, many people have experienced this phenomenon. But, regardless of the paths we take, every one of us is in receipt of spiritual guidance that is present and looks out for us at all times. Most of us are simply unaware of it...

Karmic Connections

In Hinduism, the concept of Brahman is 'the divine ground of all matter, energy, time, space, being and everything beyond in the Universe'. In the Vedas, there is a text that, when translated into English reads, 'In the beginning was Brahman, with whom was the Word, and the Word is Brahman'. This is in direct comparison to scripture that was written in the biblical Gospel of John.

In Christian doctrine, the concept of The Trinity is considered to be the unity of the Father, the Son and the Holy Spirit as three personifications in one Godhead. Embedded in ancient Brahmanism, we can find this same doctrine - the triad of Brahma the Father, Vishnu the Word and Shiva the Power.

In 563 BC, a prince named Siddhartha Gautama was born into a Hindu family in what is now modern day Nepal. Gautama is the key figure in the Buddhist religion. He was commonly known as *Buddha* - a Sanskrit word that means 'awakened one'.

Various collections of teachings attributed to the Buddha were passed down by oral tradition, but were not committed to writing until about 400 years after his death. The doctrine of the Buddha was written on parchment in the language of Pali. But what is most interesting is that there are striking similarities between the lives that both Jesus and

Buddha have led and the teachings they taught, most of which had gone completely unnoticed until the 1880's.

> **It is always the same supreme Spirit
> which embodies itself in the avatar.
> God is one without a second...
> he merely chose a different dress.**
> Swami Prabhavanada

In 1885, Professor Richard Garbe, a German Indologist and Professor of Sanskrit at the University of Tübingen in Germany, journeyed to India where he spent a year in the sacred city of Benares studying Hindu philosophy and the Sanskrit language of Hinduism and Buddhism. He then wrote a journal about his experiences. In his book, *Indien und das Christentum*, he described the many similarities he had discovered between the teachings of Hinduism and Buddhism, and those of Christianity.[21]

> **The teachings of Jesus and Buddha
> are as alike as their biographies.**
> Dr. Marcus Borg, DPhil.

Albert J. Edmunds was an early-twentieth century American scholar who graduated from the University of London. He believed that Buddhism and Christianity are one cosmic upheaval that 'burst open a crater' in India 500 years before the birth of Christ, and then a greater one around the Mediterranean Sea at the Christian Advent. Edmunds has found 112 parallels between the life and teachings of Jesus and the Buddha.[22] His meticulous two-volume work in comparative religion is titled *Buddhist and Christian Gospels*.

Karmic Connections

> **Buddhism and Christianity are two parts of one great spiritual movement.**
> Albert J. Edmunds

During the nineteenth century, the Irish antiquarian and Christian scholar, Lord Kingsborough, was the eminent authority on Mexican antiquities. A graduate of Oxford University in England, he compiled a multi-volume series, titled *Antiquities of Mexico*. It is a collection of various Mesoamerican codices that includes what historians believe to be the earliest book ever written in the Americas.[23] In his series, Lord Kingsborough outlines numerous direct correspondences between the life and teachings of Jesus and the Mayan god Quetzalcoatl, the worship of whom is documented to have begun between 400 and 600 AD.

> **There are several paintings in the *Codex Borgianus* that represent Quetzalcoatl crucified and nailed to a cross.**
> Lord Kingsborough

While there are striking similarities between the lives these great spiritual teachers have led, there are differences between their religions and Christianity today. As an example, the teachings of Hinduism and Buddhism understand the principle of *reincarnation*, which states that we are all destined to live many lives on Earth and that everyone who ascends to Heaven has already lived there. Christianity does not embrace this idea today. But this is contradictory to the first Jewish Christians who speak as though it was once common knowledge.

> **Who sinned, this man or his parents,**
> **that he was Born blind?**
> John 9:2

The fact that reincarnation is part of Jewish tradition comes as a surprise to many people. Nevertheless, it is documented, in numerous places in the ancient texts of Jewish mysticism. This includes the *Zohar*, which is a commentary on the Torah and is considered to be the most important literary work in an ancient Jewish school of thought called the Kabbalah.

> **All souls are subject to reincarnation...**
> **They do not know that they are**
> **brought before the tribunal both before they**
> **enter into this world and after they leave it.**
> Zohar II 99b

It is out of ignorance that we only believe who we remember ourselves to have been. In fact, we have lived several hundred lives incarnate in the physical form, as both women and men. But, it isn't our memories that are passed on from one life to the next, but rather, it is our Spirit. We forget our memories because the descent into matter lowers our consciousness. So the memories of the lives we have lived are lost in the same way we lose the memories of our dreams at night. Reincarnation is the long lost doctrine.

> **I will send you the prophet Elijah before that**
> **great and dreadful day of the LORD comes...**
> **"Elijah has already come**
> **and they did not recognize him..."**
> **He was talking about John the Baptist.**
> Malachi 4:5, Matthew 17:12-13

> **There has not risen anyone greater than John
> the Baptist... If you are willing to accept it,
> he is the Elijah who was to come.**
> **Matthew 11:11-14**

Isaac Newton's third Law of Motion states that, for every action, there is an equal and opposite reaction. This is the concept of living and dying 'by the sword' – the aspect of reincarnation called *karma*. It is this karmic principle that was put into place to allow us to gradually evolve to a higher state of consciousness.

> **He that leads into captivity shall go into
> captivity; he that kills with the sword
> must be killed with the sword.**
> **Revelation 13:10**

Karma has forced us to take turns playing the roles of 'good guy' and 'bad guy'. And, while playing the roles of the good guy, we have also assumed roles as victims. It has been the ultimate irony. Instead of living in paradise, we have been experiencing Time, Space and Relativity.

> **Jesus asked them, "Who do people say I am?"
> They replied, "Some say John the Baptist;
> others say Elijah; and still others,
> Jeremiah or one of the prophets."**
> **Mark 8:27-28**

Because of the principle of karma, if we manifest a pattern of negativity in our personality, our spiritual guides will use it as an opportunity to draw our attention to that negativity. The responsibility for karma is our own.

> **This Generation will certainly not
> pass away until all these things
> have happened.**
> Matthew 24:34

    Jesus' teachings indicate that two wrongs don't make things right. In other words, we should choose not to execute the murderer, but attempt instead to determine what made him a killer in the first place. So, in our many lives as victims, if we choose to forgive our aggressors, we transcend karma through God's grace and life becomes a little bit easier. As we have been learning from the roles we have played, we have been moving closer to God. Just as Hell is all around us, so is Heaven all around us.

> **For the Son of Man came to seek
> and to save what Was Lost.
> Him who overcomes I will make a
> pillar in the temple of my God.
> never Again will he leave it.**
> Luke 19:10 and Revelation 3:12

    But God has always given us the freedom to choose to incarnate, the ultimate goal of which has been to gain enough wisdom to render incarnation of no value to our spiritual growth. And, because of this cycle of Harmonic Convergence, which began in 1987, we no longer have to die to grow spiritually. We can now do so by increasing the amount of Light our cellular structures hold. Ninety-nine percent of our cells is empty Space within which exist sub-atomic bundles of energy that are traveling at the speed of Light.

> **Outwardly we are wasting away,
> yet inwardly we are being renewed
> day by day. For our Light and momentary
> troubles are achieving for us an eternal
> glory that far outweighs them all.**
> II Corinthians 4:16-17

We are all eternal Spirits that, occasionally, choose to incarnate as a physical expression. Our consciousness isn't limited to Space and Time. We are present wherever our consciousness dwells. When we are thinking about the past, our consciousness is in the past; when we are thinking about the future, we are in the future. So when we are not incarnate in the physical form, we can choose to spend an eternity guiding those who are. In this way, we are all helping to evolve humanity to a level at which we can re-experience the Eden we once knew...

Karmic Connections

Evolution of our Soul

The divine Law of Polarity states that everything is dual; everything has poles; everything has its pair of opposites; like and unlike are the same; opposites are identical in nature, but different in degree; extremes meet; all truths are but half-truths; all paradoxes may be reconciled.

Opposites are really two extremes of the same thing. Life is a circle of frequencies. There is no Hell to which 'the damned' will all be sent on Judgment Day. We already live there. We have long since descended into a lower state of consciousness in which we are trapped in ignorance and illusion in a third dimensional reality.

> **I cannot imagine a God who rewards and punishes the objects of his Creation and is but a reflection of human frailty.**
> **Albert Einstein**

Many Christians believe that, before the second coming of Christ, Satan will pretend to be God in order to deceive us all and that God is going to banish for eternity all those who are deceived. But why would He banish those people who, by innocently following Satan, are consciously trying to find God? Wouldn't our loving God be more likely to banish those who are consciously trying to turn away from Him? And why would He inflict an infinite punishment for a finite transgression? Satan isn't a being; it is a state of being.

> **Jesus turned and said to Peter,
> "Get behind me, Satan! You do not have in
> Mind the things of God, but the things of Men."**
> Matthew 16:23

Chapter 13 of the biblical *Book of Revelation* is a very revealing text. It refers to the number 666 as being the mark of 'the beast'. But, in the Periodic Table of the Elements, the atomic number for the Carbon element is six. Carbon is necessary to form all DNA and RNA, the chemical code of life as it currently exists. And the Carbon atom has six electrons, six neutrons and six protons.

> **If anyone has insight, let him
> calculate the number of the Beast,
> for it is the number of a Man.**
> Revelation 13:18

But Carbon isn't the only element that can support life. Silicon, which is the least dense of these two elements, has an electronic structure that is analogous to that of Carbon.

Dr. Max G. Lagally, BS, MS, Ph.D, is a Professor of Surface Science. In 2006, he began developing Silicon membranes in the Department of Materials Science and Engineering at the University of Wisconsin, Madison. In his research, he has discovered that the surface of a Silicon membrane can be functionalized to become pH, or biologically, sensitive. He theorizes that it could bind DNA.[24] In other words, Silicon can support life.

Materials Science is an inter-disciplinary field that studies the relationship between the structure of materials at atomic scales and their macroscopic properties. In this science, a Crystal is defined as 'a solid substance in which the atoms, molecules or ions are arranged in an orderly repeating pattern, which extends in all three Spatial dimensions'.

At the onset of World War II, a Theoretical Physicist named Dr. J. Robert Oppenheimer was working as a Professor of Physics at the University of California, Berkeley. At that time in history, there was an increasing demand for a certain type of Crystal called *quartz*, which is a naturally occurring form of Silicon. It was quartz Crystals that were used in radios that could be tuned to specific frequencies. The production of quartz frequency control Crystals rated as one of the highest U.S. military priorities, second only to atomic energy.

When Dr. Oppenheimer was just a small boy, he was fascinated by Crystals. At the age of eleven, he became the youngest member ever to join the prestigious New York Mineralogical Club when he was asked to read a paper he had written on their use. Some of his later achievements include work on electron-positron theory, quantum tunneling, relativistic quantum mechanics, quantum field theory, black holes and cosmic rays. But Dr. Oppenheimer is best remembered as being the 'Father of the Atomic Bomb'. [25]

In 1997, an Australian research team, headed by a Physicist named Dr. Bruce Cornell, Ph.D, attached a piece of foil beneath a cell membrane, and then filled the space between them with an electrolyte solution. When they stimulated the membrane's receptors with a specific frequency, the channels opened and allowed the solution across the membrane. The foil served as a transducer, which converted the electrical activity of the channels into a digital readout on a computer screen. In other words, the membranes of our cells are Crystal semi-conductors, the equivalent of Silicon micro-computer chips.[26]

In 1957, Dr. Marcel Joseph Vogel, a scientist with an Honorary Doctoral degree, joined the IBM San Jose lab as a Research Scientist where he became one of the most productive patent inventors in the history of their Data Products Division. When he began investigations into the field of liquid Crystal systems, he discovered through infrared photography that Crystals follow harmonic frequencies.[27]

After twenty-five years as a Senior Research Scientist for IBM, Dr. Vogel developed his own laboratory for building a language of identification for the subtle forces and energies that are generally considered to be metaphysical. The word *metaphysics* takes its origins from the Greek words *metá* and *physiká*, meaning 'beyond the physical'. It defines a reality that transcends those of any particular science.

Dr. Vogel's intention was to prove that science and metaphysics are intrinsically compatible. IBM donated one-half million dollars worth of equipment to his cause. Other equipment was obtained through grants from the Arthritis Foundation and donations from the Stanford Research Institute in California.

In his research, Dr. Vogel demonstrated how Crystalline growth can be modified by the patterns of human thought waves. Because thoughts travel energetically, they have a unique frequency. So, just as it is the nature of a Crystal to hold a computer software program, it is also its nature to hold a pattern of thought. In other words, it has memory.

As a result of his discovery, Dr. Vogel designed a faceted Crystal that stores, amplifies, converts and coheres subtle energies. The purpose of faceting a crystal is to amplify and transmit an increasingly coherent stream of energy. His Vogel-cut® Crystal is cut to an angle of 51 degrees, 51 minutes and 51 seconds, which is the same angle as the Great Pyramid in Egypt.[28]

> **One cannot help but be in awe when**
> **he contemplates the mysteries**
> **of eternity, of Life, of the marvelous**
> **structure of Reality.**
> **Albert Einstein**

Currently, it is water that gives us life. The most common arrangement of the Water molecule is the geometric shape of the pyramid, the Tetrahedron. The molecule of Silicon is also the Tetrahedron. But what is most interesting is that the molecule of a Silicon micro-computer chip is the shape of the Star Tetrahedron, the Star of David.

The Star Tetrahedron is the electric balance to magnetism. This is how immense amounts of data are stored so efficiently within a computer. It is the shape of the Star Tetrahedron that provides for memory. The word *memory* takes its origins from the ancient Hebrew words *mem*, which means Water, and *ohr*, which means Light.

> **No one can enter the kingdom of God
> unless he is born of Water and the Spirit...
> You must be born again.**
>
> **John 3:5-7**

Each cell in the human body contains forty-six chromosomes, which carry the genetic information needed for it to develop. Chromosomes are filled with tightly-coiled strands of DNA that, if placed end to end, would reach the Moon and back about 100,000 times.

In 1990, a group of Russian physicists, molecular biologists, biophysicists, geneticists, embryologists and linguists began a study of DNA. The research project was directed by Dr. Peter Gariaev, Ph.D, a Biophysicist and Molecular Biologist who is a member of the Russian Academy of Sciences and the Academy of Sciences in New York. During their eight year study, the researchers discovered that, independent of its function as a protein producer, our DNA is also a complex, biological, micro-computer chip. And that chip communicates with its environment.[29]

Evolution of our Soul

Dr. Gariaev found that, if the proper frequencies are used, living DNA substance in tissue will react to language-modulated laser rays. The basic structure of DNA alkaline pairs is the same as that of human language. So no DNA decoding is necessary. It can be influenced and reprogrammed solely using frequencies, without replacing genes. And it can be programmed with the frequencies of thought.

> **When we Think, we set into motion
> vibrations of a very high degree,
> but just as real as the vibrations of
> light, heat, sound, electricity.**
> **William W. Atkinson**

Dr. Bruce Lipton, Ph.D., is an internationally recognized Cellular Biologist and a pioneer in a new science called Epigenetics. In his book, titled *The Biology of Belief*, he writes that our DNA scans the environment for frequencies that are relevant to its existence, changes its structure, and then sends messages to reshape itself accordingly.[30]

The body we see in the mirror every morning, with all our thoughts and beliefs, is not who we really are. Our mind and body will die, but our Spirit is immortal. We are not products of our environment; we are influenced by it. And that environment includes our own thoughts.

Dr. Lipton also discovered that there is one characteristic that is uniform throughout the entire biosphere. This is that evolutionary advances are characterized by their ability to handle an increase in consciousness. He has found that evolution is, in fact, driven by consciousness. Dr. Lipton's book was awarded Best Science Book of the Year in 2006.

> **The greatest error which I have committed has been in not allowing sufficient weight to the direct action of the Environments, independently of natural selection.**
> **Charles Darwin**

As a joint researcher with Dr. Gariaev, Dr. Vladimir Poponin, Ph.D, is the Senior Research Scientist at the Institute of Biochemical Physics of the Russian Academy of Sciences. He is recognized worldwide as a leading expert in quantum biology, including the nonlinear dynamics of DNA and the interactions of the weak electro-magnetic fields within biological systems. In 1992, Dr. Poponin discovered that, surrounding the three-dimensional human DNA chain, there is a field structure that is inter-dimensional.[31]

Mainstream science has labeled the three-dimensional human DNA chain as the 'double-helix'. But, in its arrogance, it has also labeled as 'junk' those portions for which it has found no function. What is not yet understood by science is that, within the double-helix, there are additional double-helix strands that fuse together and add their coding into the active DNA imprint. Within our DNA, there are levels of structure and function that direct the operations of our entire genetic blueprint.

Evolution of our Soul

We all possess DNA strands that correspond to higher dimensions of consciousness. But, because only three of these strands are active, we cannot perceive of any of the higher dimensional realms. We can only perceive of three dimensions of consciousness, of a 3D reality. This prevents us from seeing the higher truths of the mind of Christ. Currently, we can only see the false reality that emerges from an anti-Christ mind.

> **Christ has indeed been raised from the dead, the first fruits of those who have fallen Asleep.**
> I Corinthians 15:20

Science is about to discover that the ninety percent of our DNA they call 'junk' is a quantum set of instructions. We are a growing global consciousness, which is capable of conscious evolution through our DNA. In spite of the fact that our current reptilian brain is fighting this process, we will soon be leaving behind our 'fight-or-flight' behavior mechanism and Darwin's struggle for existence.

> **Listen, I tell you a mystery: we will not all Sleep, but we will all be Changed.**
> I Corinthians 15:51

At this time in history, we are evolving very rapidly as a human species. The evolution of our species, the Homo sapien, is a quantum leap to an immortal species with forty-eight chromosomes and twelve active spiritual DNA strands. Our three-dimensional biology is being alchemically shifted from Carbon-based matter into that of multi-dimensional Silicon Crystal.

> **There he was transfigured before them.**
> **His face shone like the Sun,**
> **and his clothes became as**
> **white as the Light.**
> Matthew 17:2

Science is already starting to see the formation of new Crystalline structures in our pineal gland, a process they call Biomineralization. Professor Sidney B. Lang, of the Ben-Gurion University of the Negev in Israel, and Drs. Simon Baconnier and Rene de Seze of the National Institute for Industrial Environment and Risks in France, have recently discovered the presence of new microCrystals that are forming in this gland. These Crystals have piezoelectric properties with excitability in the frequency range of mobile telecommunications.[32]

Drs. Lang, Baconnier and de Seze theorize that the interaction of these Crystals with Global System for Mobile Telecommunications (GSM) waves could constitute a new mechanism of transduction on the pineal membrane.[33] GSM is a digital technology that enables up to eight telephone conversations to be held on the same channel, simultaneously.

In Hindu traditions, the pineal gland is associated with our extra-sensory third 'eye' through which perception of the world is not limited to the physical senses. The activation of these Crystals in our pineal gland is advancing us toward our multi-dimensional awareness and telepathic abilities. It is the next step in our evolution.

Internally, all our cells are being changed from an organic structure to a Silicon Crystalline structure. The Crystal is the perfect prism through which Light can pass for illumination. The speed of Light at the surface of the Earth is 186,282 statute miles per second. And this converts to 144,000 nautical miles per grid second.[34]

> **And they sang a new song before the throne... No one could learn the song except the 144,000 who had been redeemed from the Earth.**
> **Revelation 14:3**

In this evolutionary process, the whole planet is being awakened to the truth of our very existence. Light is God's Love. It is we who are 'the beast'...

Duality Consciousness

The word *holography* takes its origins from the Greek. It represents a technique that allows the Light that is scattered from an object to be recorded, and then later reconstructed as a three-dimensional image. The holograms that are seen on credit cards are etched on two-dimensional plastic film. When Light bounces off from them, it recreates the appearance of 3D.

But the real beauty of a hologram is that, if it is cut into many pieces, the entire image can still be seen on any one piece. And, if any piece is then changed, that change is reflected in each and every other piece.

> **That All of them may be One, Father,**
> **just as you are in me and I am in you...**
> **may they be brought to complete Unity.**
> **John 17:20-23**

If a beam of pure white Light is projected through a Crystal, it is diffracted as a rainbow spectrum of colors. Likewise, if that color spectrum is sent back through the Crystal, the individual frequencies will join to become that same beam of white Light.

But, if we even eliminate just one color from that color spectrum, the beam that is returned is no longer white. Each of us has a unique frequency. And God is contained in every one of us, the whole being more than merely the sum of its parts.

Duality Consciousness

> **A human being is part of the whole
> called by us Universe, a part limited in
> Time and Space. We experience ourselves,
> our thoughts and feelings as something
> separate from the rest. A kind of
> optical Delusion of Consciousness.**
> — Albert Einstein

René Descartes was a seventeenth century French Philosopher and Mathematician who many consider to be the 'Father of Modern Philosophy'. He conceived of the concept of *dualism,* which is 'the state in which we consider mind and matter to be two different things'.

As dualistic thinkers, we see life as being filled with direct opposites. As a result, we are living under the Law of Polarity, instead of fulfilling that law. And, because we have all been living in a little 'mental box', we have been incapable of seeing through this illusion.

> **The Light of the body is the eye:
> if therefore thine eye be Single,
> thy whole body shall be full of Light.**
> — Matthew 6:22

Because of the duality consciousness of humanity, we perceive ourselves as being separate from God. So we still think we must lie, cheat or steal to get what we need and want. Throughout our lives, we have believed that there are two forms of consciousness – ours and our neighbor's; ours and our spouse's; ours and our God's.

Duality Consciousness

**Because there is One loaf,
we, who are many, are One body,
for we all partake of the One loaf.**
I Corinthians 10:16-17

Dr. Jill Bolte Taylor, Ph.D, is a Neuro-Anatomist who was trained at Harvard Medical School. Her specialty is in the postmortem investigation of the human brain as it relates to schizophrenia and the other severe mental illnesses. In her book, titled *My Stroke of Insight*, she writes about her experiences in 1996, while suffering a form of arterio-venous malformation stroke, which allowed her the rare privilege of being able to study a stroke as it was actually occurring. During this stroke, she was able to watch as her own brain functions shut down, one by one - her ability to walk, talk, read and write.[35]

The swelling and trauma of the stroke placed pressure on the dominant left hemisphere of Dr. Taylor's brain. As a result, she was unable to recall any part of her life. But, in the absence of the neural circuitry of her left hemisphere, her consciousness shifted into the present moment and the functions of her right hemisphere increased. This left her feeling expansive, totally at peace in the Universe and connected as part of it.

Dr. Taylor was forced to undergo major brain surgery to remove a large blood clot that was putting pressure on her language centers. Although the stroke damaged the left side of her brain, her recovery burst forth an avalanche of creative energy from the right side. She now travels the

Duality Consciousness

country educating audiences about the beauty of the brain. In 2008, she was chosen as one of TIME Magazine's 100 Most Influential People in the World.

**I am trillions of cells
sharing a Common Mind.**
Dr. Jill Bolte Taylor, PhD

It is the split between the two hemispheres of the brain that causes us to perceive of duality. The left hemisphere is the side that is concerned only with our human condition. It understands logic, mathematics, ordered sequential relationships and the parasympathetic nervous system. Its main job has been to place everything in this reality into a Time line. This creates the illusion that we are finite.

In contrast, the right hemisphere of the brain is the side that represents the creative part of the human biology. This includes music, rhythm, imagination, intuition, humor, dreams and the sympathetic nervous system. The right hemisphere understands that we are, in fact, infinite.

**Peace is only a thought away, and all we
have to do to access it is silence the
voice of our dominating left mind.**
Dr. Jill Bolte Taylor, PhD

In the current evolution of man, it is the left hemisphere of our brain that is being adapted. This re-wiring process is establishing new synaptic pathways between the two sides, which will promote a new relationship with Space and Time. It is a process that will continue as we move toward the year 2012. The new way in which our brains will then begin to communicate will promote the end of duality.

> **To this day the same Veil remains
> when the old covenant is read.
> It has not been removed, because
> only in Christ is it taken away.**
> II Corinthians 3:14

The word *yoga* is a Sanskrit term that means 'to join'. In the Hindu philosophy, the goal of the practice of yoga is to unite ourselves with God. According to yoga, there are seven energy centers, called *chakras*, which linger between matter and Spirit. Modern science knows very little about this system, which it considers to be the autonomic nervous system.

When our chakras are functioning properly, they are open and spinning in a clockwise direction, each at a specific frequency. So a chakra is opened when its frequency is perfected. This enables it to metabolize the various energetic needs of the corresponding parts of the body. Once all seven of our chakras are perfected, they form our Tree of Life, which is an important part of the Jewish Kabbalah.

> **Blessed are those who wash their robes,
> that they may have the right to the
> Tree of Life and may go through
> the gates into the City.**
> Revelation 22:14

Duality Consciousness

Shri Mataji Nirmala Devi is a Nobel Peace Prize nominee with an Honorary Doctorate in Cognitive and Para-Psychological Sciences from the Romanian Ecological University in Bucharest. In 1970, after studying the field of medicine and focusing on the scientific terminology of the anatomy and human physiology, she started Sahaja Yoga, a philosophy of self-realization. Her yoga is now offered in over ninety countries worldwide."[36]

According to Shri Mataji, the shape of the human brain is like a prism. The energies that fall on it are refracted into four nervous systems - the left and right sympathetic, the parasympathetic and the central nervous system. During a baby's development, those energies that fall on the anterior fontanelle bone of the skull pierce it in the center, and then pass into the lower portion of the brainstem. After leaving a fine thread of divine energy there, they settle way down in the sacrum – the bone at the base of the spine.

As a baby grows, the fontanelle bone begins to calcify so that, around the age of two, the flow of divine Love is cut off from him. This causes him to identify himself as being separate from God and he begins to use his lower three chakras to obtain what he needs and wants. These lower chakras are the energies of the physical, the emotional and the mental. They are our instincts of Survival, Pro-Creation and Willpower.

Duality Consciousness

> **If there is any religion that could
> cope with modern scientific needs
> it would be Buddhism.**
> **Albert Einstein**

What science does not yet understand is that there is a gap in the parasympathetic nervous system, between the vagus nerve and the solar plexus. This is part of our genetic blueprint. In Latin, the word *vagus* means 'wandering'. As long as the child continues to identify himself as being separate from God, his consciousness will dwell in these three lower centers of energy. This is the hurdle that will limit his search for God and leave him to wander aimlessly through life.

The word *kundalini* is a Sanskrit term that means 'a coiled energy originating from the base of the spine'. There is but one bone in our bodies that is holy - the sacrum. In Greek, the word *sacrum* means 'sacred'. And it is through spiritual practices and devotion to God that the divine energy of the kundalini is awakened from our sacrum.

The job of the kundalini energy is to break up the three lower chakras. So, when it awakens, tremendous power is unleashed. The resulting expansion of consciousness affects every element of our being, from our biological functions to our personal relationships, to our concept of reality, to our influence in the world.

If this energy succeeds in rising up across the gap in the parasympathetic nervous system, it will reach the higher chakras where it will produce various degrees of spiritual enlightenment. At the level of the fourth chakra, the Heart Chakra, we will start to see divine Light. If it reaches the fifth chakra, the Throat Chakra, we find ourselves wanting to think and speak only of God.

The sixth chakra is the Pituitary Chakra. It is where the optic nerve crosses the motor nuclei fibres of the spinal nerves that serve the limbs and trunk of the body. This crossing is the most restricted path through which this holy energy can pass – the path that opens the way for our consciousness to ascend to the seventh chakra.

Enter through the narrow Gate.
Matthew 7:13

The human conditions that will prevent a person from accessing the seventh chakra are lust, greed, pride and fear. But, if the kundalini energy reaches it, we experience a vision of God and the sacred geometries with which the Universe was created. At the end of this age, we can finally experience this divine revelation, the opening of the seventh chakra – the Pineal Chakra.

The mystery... is this...
The seven lampstands are
the Seven Churches.
Revelation 1:20

The divine Law of Correspondence states that as above, so below; as below, so above. There is a symmetry between life and the various planes that exist beyond our knowing.

Duality Consciousness

The ancient Greek schema of the 'macrocosm and microcosm' sees our psychological nature as a mirror of our metaphysical nature. So the same patterns are reproduced on all levels of the cosmos, from the level of the Universe down to the level of the sub-atomic particle.

Dr. James Lovelock, B.Sc, Ph.D, D.Sc, is a Biophysicist who received his degrees from the Universities of Manchester and London. In 1961, he was employed by NASA to develop sensitive instruments for the analysis of extraterrestrial atmospheres and planetary surfaces. While working as one of their consultants, he developed the Gaia Hypothesis for which he is most widely known. Named after the Greek goddess, Gaia, this theory proposes that living and non-living parts of the Earth form a complex interacting system, which can be thought of as a single organism.[37]

The Gaia hypothesis postulates what the ancients and the indigenous people of the Earth have believed for centuries - that our planet is a vast, self-regulating intelligence, a living being. Dr. Lovelock is now a Doctor Honoris Causa of numerous universities around the world.

> **There comes a time when the mind takes**
> **a higher plane of knowledge but**
> **can never prove how it got there.**
> **Albert Einstein**

Because we are a microcosm of our living Earth, the Earth also has a kundalini energy that is grounded in its South magnetic pole – in its sacrum. For centuries, the Earth's kundalini has been located in India and Tibet. But this energy has now risen up and over the Earth and is settling in a new location - in the Mesoamerican countries. According to the Mayan prophecy of the Eagle and the Condor, this is the age when 'those of the center will unite the eagle of the North with the condor of the South'.

Just as humanity is evolving, so is the Earth in a state of evolution. It was when the indigenous tribal elders gathered in 1987, in celebration of the cycle of the Harmonic Convergence, that the Earth ascended to the next plane of existence above the physical plane, namely the astral plane – the fourth dimension.

In 2002, the Geological Survey of Canada announced that the speed at which the North magnetic pole is moving has increased considerably over the past twenty-five years and is now moving at a rate of 40 km per year.[38] It is the Earth that is leading this evolution of man.

> **Intellectualism, without a spiritual base, is a painful torture that ultimately leads to fear.**
> **Brian Eenigenburg**

Unfortunately, modern science is forever trying to discover through technology the answers that are simply revealed through spirituality. Science starts from complexity, and then shrinks down to smaller particles, or backs up to previous historical events, in a desperate search for the simple beginnings of life.

Duality Consciousness

In contrast, spiritualists innately understand the beginnings of life, which start as simplicity, and then create the wonders of complexity. The indigenous people understand this. But science still wastes a lot of time and suffers a lot of frustration trying to find through a microscope that which is easily understood through the heart. If one person follows the scientific path of quantum physics and another follows the spiritual path of the divine, they will eventually meet up and ask each other, 'Hey, how did YOU get here?'

> **All religions, arts and sciences are branches of the same tree.**
> **Albert Einstein**

In the year of this writing, another global gathering of the indigenous tribal elders took place, in an event called the Return of the Ancestors and Council of Future Wisdom Keepers. Held in Sedona, Arizona, it was a reunion of the Continental Council of Indigenous Elders of the Americas.

This major historic event encompassed ten days of ceremony and prayer, during which a new direction for the Earth was carved into nine stone tablets by over seventy tribal elders who gathered from the peaks of the Andes Mountains to the plains of Africa. And, through their wisdom, we will soon emerge from the darkness of duality into the Light of a whole new world...

The Baptism

There is much joy just ahead for humanity. But it won't come without the work that is necessary to attain Christ consciousness. And, although there are many methods of increasing our Light quotient, the best way to walk the illuminated path of the yogi is to expand our consciousness through the understanding of divine Love, wisdom and power.

> **The man who does not enter the sheep pen by the Gate, but climbs in by some other way, is a thief and a robber.**
> John 10:1

There are seven initiations that each of us must perform in order to perfect the process of yoga. The first initiation involves mastering the physical body. This is a phase of cleansing that often includes a change in diet and a reduction in exposure to toxins. Unbeknownst to me at the time, God had begun educating me in this area through the injuries and illnesses I started to experience shortly after the cycle of the Harmonic Convergence began.

The second initiation requires a level of mastery over the astral body. At this level, we become inspired by the knowledge of God and we develop a more conscious understanding of our system of spiritual guidance and of our own Spirit. This is the level at which the kundalini energy awakens and begins to rise. It is at the level where we experience the cleansing of our emotions, and then learn to control them.

> **If you hold to my teaching,
> you are really my disciples.**
>
> John 8:31

Dr. Barbara Brennan, Ph.D, is a Physicist with a Masters Degree in Atmospheric Physics from the University of Wisconsin, Madison and a former Research Scientist at NASA's Goddard Space Flight Center. In 1970, she began researching and working with the human energy field[39] – the same energy field that Bob and Don both work with.

Twelve years later, Dr. Brennan established a school of healing, which draws on both scientific and metaphysical sources to combine the aspects of the human experience that explain the process of healing. Her school is licensed by the Florida Department of Education to grant Bachelor of Science degrees in holistic healthcare. She also operates schools in Austria and Japan, both of which are specialized institutes for personal transformation.

Dr. Alberto Villoldo, Ph.D., is a Psychologist and Medical Anthropologist who founded and directed the Biological Self-Regulation Laboratory at San Francisco State University, where he studied mind-body medicine and the neuro-physiology of healing. He left his practice long ago and spent twenty-five years in the Amazon and in the Andes Mountains, in training as a shaman – a medicine man. He is the first anthropologist in America to make contact with the

The Baptism

religious leaders of the Inca tribes who live in the Andes at elevations of over 5000 meters.[40]

In his book *Mending the Past and Healing the Future*, Dr. Villoldo writes that the traditions of the Earth peoples in the Americas, Tibet, Australia and in sub-saharan Africa understand the ways of Energy Medicine. He describes how the Inca shamans use a five-thousand year old spiritual form of this medicine to work on the human energy field.

If you cut your thumb, cell division is accelerated at 1000 times its normal rate and continues until your skin grows back to exactly the same level it was at. It is the blueprint of your energy field that ensures that the regrowth does not change or alter your thumb print. The Inca shamans shift this field, which in turn gradually shifts the body, the emotions and all childhood traumas.

An essential item for the practice of shamanism is the Crystal. Imbued with a complex symbolism, Crystals are one of the most powerful tools for healing. The power of the shaman is often attributed to the presence of a Crystal, which he places on or around his body.

> **The most beautiful and most
> profound emotion we can experience
> is the sensation of the Mystical.
> It is the sower of all true Science.**
> **Albert Einstein**

One evening, Don began my appointment by using a Crystal that has a very strong affect on polarity. When all of

The Baptism

the muscles in my body went into a contracted state, I realized that it was the wrong Crystal to use at that time.

It was then that I understood what Ken had meant when he would tell me to let go of the 'steering wheel'. Unfortunately, Aries is the 'act first and ask questions or have doubts later' sign of the zodiac. We don't know how to trot. We only know how to run at a full gallop, and then limp along after getting thrown from the saddle.

I knew this incident was God's attempt at getting me to stop trying to control my life and to let Him 'take the reins'. But, because of the freedom of choice that He offered to humanity long ago, our spiritual guides must wait for a signal from us before they step forward and begin working with us from the astral plane. So, I made it known that I was putting them in charge of the healing of my physical, mental, emotional and spiritual 'bodies'.

> **When we reach a state of complete self-surrender to divine providence, God guides our every step.**
> **Swami Prabhavananda**

Dr. Hal H.E. Puthoff, Ph.D, is a Physicist in Quantum Electro-dynamics and the Director of the Institute for Advanced Studies at Austin, a private think tank established in 1985 to explore advanced concepts at the forefront of science. Following a sabbatical at Stanford University to obtain his Ph.D., he founded what was then a highly-classified, but now highly-publicized program called

The Baptism

STAR GATE, which was funded by the CIA, DIA and various military organizations.[41]

Dr. Puthoff frequently makes reference to early-twentieth century experiments in which an airless vacuum was used as a means to determine if there is energy in empty Space. This vacuum was lead-shielded from all known electro-magnetic fields. When it was cooled down to the temperature where all matter is supposed to stop vibrating and produce no heat, a tremendous amount of energy was found to exist. Because this energy can exist at absolute zero, it has come to be known as Zero Point Energy, a source of power that has more than enough strength to sustain the existence of all physical matter.[42]

Dr. Ervin Laszlo, Ph.D, is a former Professor of Philosophy who holds the highest degree of the State Doctorate, is the recipient of four Honorary Ph.Ds and was nominated for the 2004 Nobel Peace Prize. In his book, titled *Science And The Akashic Field*, he writes extensively about a Zero Point Energy called the Akashic field – a field that stores everything that has ever occurred in life, on Earth and in the cosmos. It is the original source of all things that arise in Space and Time, and it relates to everything in our future.

Akash is a Sanskrit word that means 'the essence of all things in the material world'. Also referred to as 'the ethers', akash does not travel along the normal curvatures of Space and Time; it is a pattern that is traveling in a

The Baptism

frictionless state. As part of the human energy field, akash can also be found stored in our Crystalline DNA spirals. It is akash that Bob and Don access when they use the science of Applied Kinesiology to ask for information about the body.

> **But when he, the Spirit of truth, comes,**
> **he will guide you into all truth.**
> **He will not speak on his own; he will speak**
> **only what he Hears, and he will**
> **tell you what is yet to come.**
> **John 16:13**

This 'cellular memory' contains records of every experience you have had in all your lifetimes on Earth - every thought, action and emotion. You have access to this information. It is your birthright. And anyone who is given the authority to do so can also access it. This includes your spiritual guides – those who have passed on and now live multi-dimensionally between incarnations.

> **And I saw the dead, great and small, standing**
> **before the throne, and books were opened.**
> **Another book was opened,**
> **which is the Book of Life.**
> **Revelation 20:12**

When your spiritual guides perform 'readings' of your akash, they see your lives as an analogous horserace, within which each of the horses in the race is a reflection of you. If you imagine the past, present and future as the horses in the race, you can understand how they view all of your lives at once. Each horse is a life you are living, have lived or might live. Time does not exist in the higher dimensions of

The Baptism

consciousness. As a result, your guides can see all of your 'horses' simply by looking down on the 'track'.

If you visualize your guides scanning the horse that is in the lead, and then you imagine them producing an enormous bar graph of all the frequencies it carries within it, you can see how they can identify all the strengths and weaknesses of your physical, mental, emotional and spiritual bodies simply by examining the highest and lowest bars on the graph. And this is all done in real-time.

> **The human body is literally**
> **a gigantic liquid Crystal.**
> **Dr. Robert O. Becker, MD**

In his clinic, Don stores over one-hundred frequencies that are used exclusively to treat human emotions. These frequencies resonate with every emotion a person can ever have. Because I had handed the control of my healing over to my spiritual guides, they instructed him to treat me for the frequency of every one of those emotions. He was told to open each case of vials, and then place them in my hand with the vials still intact. Although he had attended numerous seminars on this type of reprogramming, he had never seen anyone do anything like this. The next morning, I felt like running in the snow and exchanging gifts.

> **Unless you change and become like**
> **little children, you will never enter**
> **the Kingdom of Heaven.**
> **Matthew 18:3**

The Baptism

I was sure that when most of the incoherent emotions I had held were gone, there would be nothing left but peace, love and joy. But, three days later, I found myself feeling completely empty. I didn't feel sad; nor did I feel particular joyful. I felt neutral - like I was in a void. When I told this to Don, my guides instructed him to treat me for the frequency of *Detachment*, the dictionary definition of which is 'showing lack of emotional involvement'.

I was confused at to exactly why I was feeling this way. So I asked God to reveal the reason to me. Almost instantly, I regained a long lost memory of a time in my childhood when my eldest sister was visiting. She was in the final stages of pregnancy with her second son when one of my three brothers returned home after living out of town for many months. Surprised to see her condition, he asked her when she was due to deliver.

Even at eight years of age, I found it very odd that my parents hadn't informed my brother that he would soon be an uncle. By drawing on this forgotten memory, God revealed to me just how detached my family really is. At that moment, it became clear to me that my perception of life growing up in Happy Swell Meadows has, in fact, been an illusion.

I am the youngest of six children. When I was a teenager, my brother moved to California where he became engaged, and then married. When the Gulf War began, he

The Baptism

and his wife moved back to Canada. But the rest of us rarely took the time to visit them and they rarely visited any of us. We were detached.

When I was just a toddler, my eldest brother moved away from home. After that, we only heard from him every ten years or so. Eventually, he had a child with a woman I have never met. He was detached.

When I was about twelve years old, my eldest sister became angry with her son's school for forcing him to adopt Christian views by insisting that he read the Bible. I informed her that she behaved the same way whenever she tried to force the rest of us to adopt her views by insisting that we read the writings of Ayn Rand. My sister disappeared from our lives after that day. She was detached.

When I had started making plans to move to the Gulf Islands, my daughter said to me, "Won't you be lonely living there all by yourself?" But I wasn't worried about being lonely. I was detached. My entire family is detached - from our mother and father, from each other and, most importantly, from God. We all pride ourselves on being independent people. But, in reality, it is just a form of detachment, a form of the duality consciousness.

I was a teenager when my parents told the youngest of my brothers that he would have to pursue an occupation

The Baptism

or leave home. A few weeks later, we received news that he had committed suicide. He was detached.

My parents had passed down to us their separation from God, one that had likely been passed down from their own parents. They loved all of us and they loved each other. But they never emphasized a lot of physical closeness and emotional openness. And they never spoke to us about God. The only one of us who had managed to avoid this condition was my sister, Lynn, who had been blessed to find God at the age of nine.

Soon after God revealed this family issue to me, my spiritual guides suggested I take the essence of the Bush Gardenia flower. The definition for that essence is, 'For renewing passion and interest in family relationships; to draw together those who are moving away from one another, busy in their own world; to turn one's head to see what their family members are doing and feeling; to discover what is needed to bring them back together'. Then, I was treated for the frequency of *Forgiveness of Self*.

> **When the solution is simple,
> God is answering.**
> **Albert Einstein**

At this point in my initiation, I started to raise the levels of my frequencies through self-awareness. I wanted to increase the amount of Light in my cellular structures. So I actively began searching for ways to help me accomplish this.

The Baptism

I purchased a library of books on religion and spirituality and several film documentaries. I began listening to the music of Enigma – an inspirational music project that began in the 1990s. I watched every movie about Jesus Christ and the four gospels that I could find. And Ken would patiently watch them all with me.

God kept directing me to various sources of information in an effort to accelerate my awakening process. I was being drawn to read everything spiritual I could get my hands on. I began to understand why Lynn spent the majority of her free time reading the Bible. Following God was like following the Light of the White Yarrow.

As I practiced spiritual disciplines, my desire to realize God became intensified until it was a raging hunger and a burning thirst. I never considered meditation because my mind was always on God. All I talked about was God and all I cared about was what is holy.

> **In your exploration of Bible Truth,**
> **see to it that you do not rest satisfied**
> **in the yellow clay of a few spiritual**
> **discoveries, but press on to the**
> **rich blue clay underneath.**
> **Emmet Fox**

By this time, whenever I walked through an 'open door', there would be ten new doors to have to walk through. But, it would take only a few days before I could walk through all ten doors simultaneously. The rate at which

The Baptism

knowledge was being given to me was increasing exponentially.

God was answering my prayers much more quickly now. Whenever I questioned something, I would pray to Him before falling asleep at night. By morning, in the shallow REM state that exists just before we awaken, He would reveal the answer to me. That is the only time the left and right hemispheres of our brain work together harmoniously. It is then that I would receive a word, a phrase, a song, a dream, a vision or a memory.

Whenever I would become aware of something profound, God would behave even more profoundly. Sometimes, He would super-impose multiple memories overtop of one another. A single image creates a picture. But multiple images can tell a tale. This was one of the amazing methods He would use to change my perspectives on life.

> **But seek first his kingdom and his righteousness, and all these things will be given to you as well.**
> **Matthew 6:33**

When I asked God to reveal to me the reason why I am such a Doubting Thomas, almost immediately He super-imposed for me three long lost memories. These super-imposed memories told a story of some older girls who had bullied me on three separate occasions when I was of the ages six, twelve and thirteen. I had never seen the correlation between these three separate incidents before.

The Baptism

But God clearly showed me that, like many other people, this pattern of victimization had affected me to such an extent that I have been living my entire life with a belief that something bad is always going to happen.

One night, I asked God why I always felt an overwhelming urge to punish those who cause me to have ill feelings, even though I know that doing so will cause me regrets. In the early morning hours, I awoke to the song *Husbands and Wives*, which was playing in my head. The song is sung by Neil Diamond, one of pop music's most enduring and successful singer-songwriters. The part of the song God played to me is sung 'It's my belief pride is the chief cause of the decline in the number of husbands and wives'. It is our pride that makes us feel the need to punish the people who cause us grief.

> **The Counselor, the Holy Spirit...**
> **will remind you of everything**
> **I have said to you.**
> **John 14:26**

First published in 1923, *The Ego and the Id* is a prominent paper written by Dr. Sigmund Freud as an analytical study of the human psyche. It is of fundamental importance in the development of psycho-analytic theory. In his paper, Freud wrote that the *id* is our conscious, the *ego* is our sub-conscious and the *super-ego* is our Spirit.[43]

As an information processor, the conscious mind can only process forty bits of information per second. But the sub-conscious mind is one million times more powerful. It is

The Baptism

the sub-conscious mind that stores the past but lives in the present. So it is this mind that continuously replays in the present the events that have taken place in the past.

According to Dr. Sonia Choquette, the first step in connecting with our Spirit is to quiet the ego who lives in our sub-conscious. She describes the ego as 'the one who rants, blames, defends, judges, justifies, whines, doesn't forgive, never forgets, expects the worst and trusts no one'.

> He will give you another Counselor
> to be with you forever — the Spirit of Truth.
> The world cannot accept him, because it neither
> sees him nor knows him. But you know him,
> for he lives with you and will be in you.
> John 4:16-17

Dr. Candace Pert, Ph.D, is a Neuroscientist and a former Research Professor in the Department of Physiology and Biophysics at the Georgetown University School of Medicine. She is well known in the scientific community for her discovery of opiate receptors that exist in the brain. In her book, *Molecules of Emotion*, she writes that there are numerous vibrating receptors on the surface of each of our cells. They are designed to respond to neuropeptides that transmit specific instructions to those cells. They carry information in a vast network that links matter with the non-material world of the psyche.

> Your body is your subconscious mind.
> Dr. Candace Pert, PhD

The Baptism

Your Spirit is still merged with God. So it is your Spirit that is carrying out God's divine plan for you. Often referred to as the Higher Self, your Spirit carries with it the faculties of clairvoyance, clairaudience, clairsentience and intuition. Stored in a quantum state in your Crystalline DNA, it is the multi-dimensional part of you that never 'left the Garden'. And your sub-conscious mind is the gateway to it. So we need to clear any incoherent energies from our sub-conscious if we want to connect with our Spirit.

> **The man who enters by the Gate**
> **is the shepherd of his sheep.**
> **The watchman opens the Gate for him,**
> **and the sheep listen to his voice.**
> John 10:2-3

As spring turned into summer, sexual stereotyping and exploitation started to bother me. This is a topic that had not been much of a problem for me in the past. But, at the level I was at in the initiation process, I began to realize that, at some point in history, certain boundaries were placed around women that have not been placed around men. And many women have come to accept these boundaries and actively promote them within themselves. This is a condition I have come to refer to as *ornamentalism*.

> **Your beauty should not come from**
> **outward adornment... it should be that**
> **of your inner self, the unfading beauty**
> **of a gentle and quiet Spirit, which is**
> **of great worth in God's sight.**
> I Peter 3:3-4

The Baptism

The first issue of Playboy magazine was published in the 1950's. The women of the 60's and 70's attempted to end this type of sexism by taking a stand on the issue during the Women's Liberation Movement. Recently, DOVE soap has started a global effort to help women all over the world free themselves from these stereotypes.

At the time of this writing, DOVE's Campaign for Real Beauty and Self-Esteem was focusing on how teenage girls are constantly being bombarded with unrealistic, unattainable messages and images of beauty and sexuality, which severely impact their self-esteem. Their advertising is using thought-provoking ads to target society's small-mindedness.

> **Teenaged girls are the most depressed group in the UK. We must end this insanity.**
> **Lynn McTaggart**

DOVE is currently working with the entertainment industry to offer self-esteem workshops for mothers and daughters. They have released a film, titled *Onslaught*, which dramatizes the barrage of sexual stereotypical images that girls face today. The goal of their campaign is to truly make a difference in the lives of at least five million girls.

> **One hundred and sixty years ago, women helped to forge this frontier. They weren't something to be painted, pierced, tattooed and patted on their fannies, and then sent out into the world as an ornament or trophy.**
> **Dr. Craig Lampe, PhD**

The Baptism

In the language of ancient Hebrew, the word *woman* is translated as two pictures that signify 'mighty' and 'warrior'. The pioneer women I wrote about in my books about the Gulf Islands were women of relentless determination, whose tenacity helped them to conquer loneliness and poverty. Their work was the work of survival. It demanded as much from them as it demanded from the men they wed.

> **Because man hasn't accepted his own divinity, he cannot see that same divinity in woman. This creates a discontentment in her soul and she wonders if she will ever be loved in the way that is her birthright.**
> **Peter Archer**

The divine Law of Gender states that gender is in everything; everything has its masculine and feminine principles; gender manifests on all planes. Man needs to realize that he, too, has felt this same discontentment while living many, many lives as women. And, in his current life, he will feel it again as he watches his daughters grow. In this age, women will need to take back their sexuality and exchange it for their rightful positions as mighty warriors in this world.

> **And the two will become One Flesh.**
> **So they are no longer two, but One.**
> **Mark 10:8**

One of the biggest dimensional shifts people will experience during this evolution is the dimension of sleep. As our emotions start to open up, our bodies will attempt to

The Baptism

balance themselves. This will manifest itself as hot flashes and night sweats, and often very vivid and sometimes incoherent dreams.

Over the next few years, there will be increasing emotional depression on this planet. Because repression of energy is the greatest problem in the world, we will become more sensitive than ever before. We have been trained to repress our feelings of love and compassion. But it is compassion that fills us with Light. If we hold back our tears, we miss out on an opportunity to increase our quotient of Light.

Because of the increased levels of Light I was starting to carry, all of the parts of me that were not loved began to rise to the surface to be cleansed and healed. Ken would try to comfort me by telling me that God does not expect us to become saints overnight.

My guides suggested I take flower essences to help provide relief from the symptoms in my physical body, to help me bring all of the functions of my metabolic system into complete balance and harmony, and to help me restore my cells to efficient functioning. I was also taking essences to cleanse me of certain emotions. Flower essences are tinctures of liquid consciousness and stored within them is an evolutionary force that is shaped to a specific pattern.

As my mental body toggled between surrendering to God and holding back out of fear of losing control, I felt like I

The Baptism

was walking between two worlds, without an identity and without friends who understood. I was beginning to go through the same initiation process that Ken had gone through while he had attended the AA program.

When I asked my guides if I could divulge the information I was learning to my friends and family members, they simply said, *"Chill!"* I felt like I was leading the life of a secret agent. Luckily, Ken understood. He is the strongest person I have ever met.

> **These are they who have come out of the great tribulation; they have washed their robes and made them white in the blood of the Lamb.**
> **Revelation 7:14**

By this time, I had given up all my past beliefs and completely adopted new ways of perceiving reality. I started to dismantle my old ways of operating, in favor of more spiritual ways. I realized that I was part of a divine plan and a force of evolution.

Placing God's divine plan first had become foremost in my mind. I knew I had to master my thoughts, feelings and actions. I had to maintain my consciousness at a frequency of between 734 Hz and 1000 Hz. This is the state of consciousness that builds the foundation for greatness. This is the path of the yogi – the Buddhic path.

As I learned to walk this path, I started experiencing God's grace. And, while in this state of peaceful bliss, I

The Baptism

would study my pet Dachshunds. To our male, our female is not only a playmate, friend and lover, she is also his sister and his mother. He does not ponder where he came from; nor does he plan where he's going. He simply lives his life eternally in God's grace – the Tao!

> **Look deep into Nature, and then you will understand everything better.**
> **Albert Einstein**

Each of us has an entourage of twelve spiritual beings who are with us during our incarnation. Some of them belong to three spheres of angelic beings of Light who serve as counselors, governors and messengers. Now that humanity has entered a time of increased awareness, these angelic beings are no longer guarding us; they are becoming our guides to greater consciousness. As we seek to follow the ways that are most aligned with God, they are drawn to begin working with us as individuals. And the moment we make the conscious decision to dedicate our lives to Him, they dedicate themselves fully to us.

> **The harvest is the End of the Age, and the Harvesters are Angels.**
> **Matthew 13:39**

During one of my usual Friday appointments, my guides did something they had never done before. They told Don to treat me for the frequencies of *Quarrels* and *Cluttering*. They said, "Your spiritual name is SHA-HA-LAH. You are going to be an Oracle and we are sorting out in your future who will be working with you in this process."

The Baptism

Soon, there was a group of angelic beings working with me called Angels and Virtues. The Angels are those who work closest to us and the Virtues send out massive amounts of divine energy to us. Because their true names are sung in Light, this group simply calls themselves, 'Themselves'. I wondered why they would have wings, since if they move at the speed of Light, wings would just slow them down. But what we perceive as their wings are actually intricate traces of fibers of energy.

I told Don that I would need to know how to spell the beautiful spiritual name they had given me. When I later revisited the little bookstore, my Angels led me to find a paperback that revealed its spelling. It was printed in all capital letters deep inside the book.

That little bookstore became a source of sacred information for me. As a researcher and historian, my desire for knowledge about the history of mankind had become insatiable. So, I would ask God to reveal something to me, and then visit the bookstore. There, I would be led to the book that held the answer. Coincidences had become 'the norm'.

> **There is nothing concealed
> that will not be disclosed, or hidden
> that will not be made known.**
> **Matthew 10:26**

It was my Angels who suggested I resume writing. At that time, I was unsure as to whether it was for the sake of those who might read my writing or simply for the sake of my own creativity. But I knew that, in this age, God is leading us to a state of mind that I have come to call the *Mennonite Mentality*.

The Mennonites are a group of Christian Anabaptist denominations whose teachings are imbued with the Spirit of the Sermon on the Mount. It has an emphasis on peace, love, community and service, the beauty of which is that, if someone in the group is in need, the entire community comes together in service to them. This is also the final step in the AA program, which requires from its members that, after having had a spiritual awakening as the result of completing the steps in the program, they carry 'the message' to others who are in need.

Researching and writing the history of the Gulf Islands had all been done in preparation for the time when I would piece together my own history in the writing of this book. Writing made me feel spiritually alive. As this book came together, I began to feel whole again. All of the fragmented parts of me were beginning to come back together. But this isn't my story; it is the story of my Spirit.

My Angels would later say, *"You are destined to become a teacher and a healer."* For seven years, while I taught in a classroom, I had led a healthy and happy life. But as soon as I shifted the direction of that life, my health broke down in preparation for the role I would play as a healer. This is the other role my Spirit had planned for me in this age.

The Baptism

> **To one there is given through the Spirit
> the message of wisdom, to another
> the message of knowledge by means of
> the same Spirit... to another, gifts of
> healing by that one Spirit.**
> 1 Corinthians 12:8-9

Eventually, Ken and I started using Applied Kinesiology to muscle test one another. He would ask questions of my Spirit that helped me determine which flower essences, supplements and homeopathic remedies I should be taking. When I finished writing this book, he used me as a surrogate to determine which of my friends and family members were ready to read it. The details of this book fit together like a glove because they are the truth. But some people are not yet ready for this truth.

One day, I discovered a vial into which had been infused quantum instructions that download frequencies from anywhere in the Akashic field. These instructions are stored energetically, in a form in which they can be interpreted by the body.

When the vial is placed on the thymus gland, it is moved into the human energy field where the body energetically 'runs' the instructions like a macro. Because it controls the acupuncture energy meridians, the thymus gland is responsible for the regulation of energy through this energy field. It can initiate instantaneous corrections to overcome energetic imbalances. It is the link between the mind and the body.

The Baptism

With the help of my Angels, Don and I learned how to infuse over one-hundred different instructions into this vial, which we then began to mass produce for his clients. Each vial universally helps to address the needs of people who are suffering from practically any physical ailment or emotional imbalance, ranging from asthma to addictions and from Obsessive Compulsive Disorder to Irritable Bowel Syndrome.

Don determines the frequencies that are needed by his clients, and then I 'program' a vial for them so they can download the necessary frequencies themselves, as they require them. This also applies to most of the homeopathic, herbal, ayurvedic and allopathic remedies and flower essences on the planet. This discovery is a quantum leap in Energy Medicine. Everything belongs to God.

> **If there is a natural body,
> there is also a spiritual body.**
> 1 Corinthians 15:44

One morning, while Ken was driving to his job site, a large white butterfly appeared out of thin air and hovered above the passenger seat of his truck. It then flew past his head and out of the window. He thought he was hallucinating but, a few days later, it happened again.

The following week, we took our dogs down to a rocky beach near our home. While he was standing near the edge of the water, a polished semi-precious stone, called *charoite*, washed up at his feet. It was a Crystal. At that time, Ken was being guided by the consciousness of an

The Baptism

elderly man and a gypsy woman from ancient Egypt. They told him he was receiving good omens. The butterfly represented transformation. They said to him, *"You are going to be a shaman. Everything you have been through in your life has prepared you for this change."*

> **For you were once darkness,**
> **but now you are Light in the Lord.**
> **Ephesians 5:8**

If the horse that is winning your multi-dimensional 'horserace' falls behind, or if it strays off the track your Spirit has laid out for you, your system of spiritual guidance will place obstacles in your life. They will do this in a deliberate attempt to lead you back onto the track. And the harder you resist their guidance, the more obstacles they will place in your way. This is how most people come to find God. When their lives become hopeless, they finally look to Him to remove the obstacles...

The Baptism

for you were once darkness,
but now you are Light in the Lord.

There is No Spoon

Science has identified all of the seven divine laws, with one exception - that of the Law of Mind. This law states that mind may be transmuted, from state to state; degree to degree; condition to condition; pole to pole; vibration to vibration. This law became evident to Dr. Marcel Vogel when he discovered that, if he tore a leaf from one plant, a second plant would respond, but *only* if he was paying attention to it.

> **If a tree falls in a forest and
> no one is around to hear it,
> does it make a sound?**
> **Bishop George Berkley**

The University of California, Berkeley was named after Bishop George Berkeley, an eighteenth century Irish Philosopher. His primary philosophical achievement was the advancement of a theory called Subjective Idealism, which suggests that we cannot know if an object truly exists; we can only know if it is perceived by our mind.

In 1925, a Theoretical Physicist named Dr. Werner Heisenberg developed a theory that has come to be known as the Heisenberg Uncertainty Principle. This theory states that an observer influences the outcome of events simply by observing them. In other words, it is only if we expect to see a sub-atomic particle in a specific location that it will exist there.

There is No Spoon

In 1968, Dr. Amit Goswami, Ph.D., became a member of the Institute for Theoretical Physics. He is now a Professor Emeritus of Physics at the University of Oregon, as well as the author of *Quantum Mechanics*, a university textbook that is used in countries all over the world. His idealist interpretation of quantum mechanics was partially inspired by the Vedanta philosophy.[44]

There is a metaphysical theory, called Monistic Idealism, which is central to the Vedanta philosophy. It states that it is consciousness, not matter, which is the foundation for everything. There is only one thing in the Universe - consciousness. If we close our eyes, does the world still exist even though we are not conscious of it? According to Dr. Goswami and a growing number of other physicists around the world, the answer is 'No'.

> **Reality is merely an Illusion,
> albeit a persistent one.**
> **Albert Einstein**

Over the past decade, a team of researchers at Princeton University has been conducting experiments to measure the effects of human consciousness when focused on random events. Called the Global Consciousness Project, this initiative is an international effort involving computers at sixty-five sites around the world, each using 'random number generators'. The purpose of this experiment is to examine subtle correlations that reflect the presence and activity of the consciousness of humanity.

There is No Spoon

The results of this project generally show completely random numbers. But, when a global event receives the focused attention of a large group of people, the numbers on the computer graphs suddenly become non-random. Major events that have coincided with this dramatic change include global meditations, major earthquakes and even the funeral for Princess Diana. But the strongest effect of this was demonstrated when people worldwide were focused, in unified consciousness, on the events of the disaster at the World Trade Center on September 11, 2001.[45]

> **Sept 11 was in the middle of the graph,**
> **and the spike just sits there all by itself,**
> **mocking us in our ignorance of what it means.**
> **Dr. Dean Radin, PhD**

The Director of the project, Dr. Roger Nelson, Ph.D, served as the Coordinator of Research at the Engineering Anomalies Research laboratory at Princeton University until his recent retirement. He is currently participating with a group of materials scientists, physicists, neurologists and biologists, in an initiative called The Intention Experiment. This project consists of a series of web-based initiatives involving thousands of people around the world in an attempt to scientifically measure the power of the human mind. These initiatives are the largest mind/matter experiments in the world.

The Global Coherence Initiative is a similar project that has recently been established, the goal of which is to unite people in focused intention, in an effort to shift global consciousness from instability and discord to balance, cooperation and peace. The researchers state that meditation, prayer, affirmation and intention affect the world, and that they can be even more effective by adding 'heart coherence' - a state of energetic alignment and cooperation between the emotional, mental, physical and spiritual bodies.

The Global Coherence Initiative project is a collaborative research initiative between the Institute of HeartMath, Dr. Elizabeth Rauscher and several other engineers and scientists to design, build and maintain multiple sensors around the world, which will directly measure fluctuations in the magnetic fields generated by the Earth. This sensing technology will allow researchers to observe changes in the Earth's magnetic field in an effort to determine if it is affected by our intentions.

Because we are divine, there is a power that is produced when two or more people are gathered together in focused intention. This phenomenon, which is called the Third Force, alchemically creates a third energy that operates outside the concept of Time.

> **For where two or three come together in my name, there am I with them.**
> **Matthew 18:20**

As the first signs of fall began to appear, I decided to return to my little bookstore. There, I was led to find yet another interpretation of the Sermon on the Mount. The author was Emmet Fox, one of the most influential authors of the New Thought movement. If a person reads just two books in his entire lifetime, it should be the versions of this sermon, which have been written by the Hindu Swami Prabhavananda and by the New Thought philosopher Emmet Fox.

The New Thought philosophy developed as a spiritual movement largely as the result of Orthodox Christianity, Unitarian Sensationalism and Transcendentalism. It promotes the concept of mind/matter to emphasize the fact that divinity dwells within each of us and that we are all spiritual beings.

We are not human beings having a spiritual experience. We are spiritual beings having a human experience.
Teilhard de Chardin

In his book, Fox wrote that matter is finite, that it is the raw material by which God individualizes Himself. Through the power of conscious prayer, God has given man the power to manifest what he wants and needs on the material plane. It is God who does the work and we are the channels through which His divine actions take place.

Our role in the manifestation is simply to forget about the work in the knowledge that He has already taken care of it. As long as we don't feel the need to control the way in which God answers our prayers, His magic will work. God already knows how to proceed. He just requires a vehicle of matter through which he can work. He just wants our Light.

There is No Spoon

**I said You are Gods;
you are all Sons of the Most High.**
Psalm 82:6

Shortly after reading Fox's book, I awoke from a dream in which I was playing a game of Cops 'n Robbers with three faceless people. In this dream, I would point my finger, just like children do when they pretend their hand is a gun. I would aim my pretend gun at the three faceless people, and then shoot. When I later ran up to them to see if they were hurt, one of them stood up and said, "Wow! That felt just like a soft breath of air."

This dream was the way in which God chose to show me that the manifestation of what we want on the material plane is accomplished through a harmless game He wants us all to play. God created us to be co-creators with Him. We just have to 'take aim and shoot'. Words of prayer are words of power. They compel matter to shape itself. Man gains dominion over this Earth when he realizes this.

But if we set a prayer in motion, the Law of Mind requires that we also expect that we have, in fact, set it in motion. Only if we believe a sub-atomic particle will exist in a specific location will it exist there. This ancient law is the magic of God's universe that we have long since forgotten.

**Whatever you ask for in prayer,
Believe that you have received it,
and it will be yours.**
Mark 11:24

Out of sheer faith, Ken then visited our local casino to apply the principles of the Law of Mind. He placed five one-hundred dollar bills all in a row along the top of one of the digital slot machines, and then literally began speaking to the machine aloud. First, he pointed at the five bills and said, "These are all one-thousand dollar bills." Then, he proceeded to command the wildcards to move to the winning side of the screen.

Within a few minutes, Ken turned his initial five-hundred dollar investment into a five-thousand dollar windfall. And, after only three weeks of playing the slot machines, he won roughly twenty-thousand dollars simply by using his mind to move matter.

> **If you have faith as small as a mustard seed,**
> **you can say to this mountain,**
> **'Move from here to there,' and it will move.**
> **Nothing will be impossible for you.**
> **Matthew 17:20**

Ken is the owner of a successful home renovation business. In a past incarnation, he had been directly involved in the building of Solomon's temple, which was constructed for the Jews in ancient Israel. But, just before Christmas, he started to sink into a depression because many of his clients simply didn't want to pay their final bill. So I felt compelled to say a heartfelt prayer for him. Because of the high degree of Light I was holding, his counselor from Alcoholics Anonymous called him long-distance only minutes later. During their conversation, he said to Ken, "I was told to call." Ken hadn't spoken to him in years.

At my appointment that evening, Don looked at me and said, *"Do you feel the power that is being given to you?"* Most people only pray when they are desperate and in need. But it is when our frequencies are held at a high level that we step into our power. That is the time to pray for whatever it is we need and want. That is the time when our prayers are most powerful.

> **Did I not tell you that if you Believed,
> you would see the glory of God?**
> **John 11:40**

One day, Ken was stretching my neck and a joint between my shoulder blades popped out of place. I thought he had performed the stretch incorrectly so I was angry with him for a week. During that week, I attended four appointments with my local chiropractor. But the joint wouldn't stay in place. When I began to suspect that this was another important spiritual lesson I needed to learn, I forgave Ken, cancelled all my upcoming appointments, and then simply asked God to take care of it.

The following day, that joint magically moved itself back into place. As soon as I gave up my willpower to God, He solved the problem for me. All it took was faith and conscious prayer – the same form of prayer Lynn had been using her entire life. I was actually performing the miracles Jesus had said we can perform.

There is No Spoon

> **Anyone who has faith in me will do what
> I have been doing. He will do even
> greater things than these.**
> John 14:12

That night, God sang to me another Neil Diamond song. The song is called *Play Me* and the part He sang is sung, 'I am the Sun; you are the Moon. I am the words; you are the tune... Play!' In the weeks that followed, my joint popped out of place several times. Each time, I would simply use conscious prayer to rectify the problem.

> **It is the Father, living in me,
> who is doing his work.**
> John 14:10

Early in the New Year, the client for whom Ken was in the middle of completing a large renovation job suddenly canceled all renovations. At that time, Ken desperately tried to apply the Law of Mind to manifest the funds we needed to pay our monthly bills. It was then that we realized that faith alone isn't enough to master this law. We must first free ourselves from all incoherent energies, such as grief, worry and fear. It is a pure heart to which matter responds. We have all been using the wrong equation. It isn't mind/matter; it is heart+faith/matter.

> **If I have a faith
> that can move mountains,
> but Have Not Love, I am nothing.**
> I Corinthians 13:1-2

The divine Law of Causation states that every cause has its effect; every effect has its cause; everything happens according to law; chance is but a name for law not recognized; there are many planes of causation, but nothing escapes the Law.

Followers of the New Thought movement firmly believe in and faithfully practice this law. One of the early thinkers of the philosophy was William W. Atkinson who, in 1906, wrote a book titled *Thought Vibration: or the Law of Attraction in the Thought World*. The basic premise behind the teachings of this book is that our thoughts create our reality. In other words, if we believe a sub-atomic particle will exist in a specific location, it will exist there. This is the principle that allows conscious prayer to work. But this principle also applies to *unconscious* prayer.

Prayer is both a science and an art.
Emmet Fox

Dr. Joshua David Stone, Ph.D, was a late-twentieth century Psychologist and the author of numerous works on Spiritual Psychology and Integrated Ascension, a term he coined to stress the importance of mastering and integrating the mind and emotions with the spiritual path. In his book, titled *The Universal Laws of God*, he wrote about how we are all electro-magnetic beings. So our sub-conscious mind is always attracting and magnetizing frequencies.

Every thought produces a unique tone. So every thought has its own unique frequency. Once a thought is accepted into the conscious mind, it imprints itself on the sub-conscious like a computer, which then attracts and magnetizes it. As a result, our thought waves are frequencies to which other similar frequencies are constantly resonating.

We are consciously and unconsciously broadcasting frequencies that are picking up similar frequencies from everyone and everything around us. We are literally attracting frequencies back to ourselves like a magnet. This is the basis for a universal principle called *attraction*. God's Universe is a 'magic mirror'.

There is nothing outside of God, who is in everything. But, as human beings, it is we who have been created in His image. And, that image is imprinted in our Crystalline DNA spirals. We are the only living things that have the capacity to change matter with our own thoughts.

> **You have taken off your old self with its practices and have put on the new self, which is being renewed in Knowledge in the image of its Creator.**
> **Colossians 3:9-10**

Whenever Ken would pick me up from my appointments with Don, he would park his truck in the parking lot beside Don's clinic. One evening, as we were driving away from the clinic, I began to feel electric shocks in the heel of my left hand. My Angels later said, *"Someone who was feeling confused and out of control had been lingering around Ken's truck while it was parked."*

The darker electro-magnetic frequencies of the person's thoughts had been attracted to Ken's dark-colored truck. When I got into his truck, I was able to feel them because of the high levels of Light I was carrying. We are the only living things that have the capacity to resonate with every vibration around us.

> **The spiritual key to the Bible is the knowledge that the entire outer world... is amenable to the energy of our Thoughts.**
> **Emmet Fox**

While Don was tearing around the clinic, my Angels said to him, *"You don't have to hurry back to tend to Vicky; you and she have now transcended Time."* I had raised my quotient of Light, which had caused my spiritual body to cross into the higher dimensions where Time does not exist. It is through this same altering of Time that yogis comprehend the divine.

In the third dimension, there is a long delay between our causes and the effects. But, in the fourth dimension, the Spatial context is less dense. Particles move faster and are spaced farther apart. So Light travels faster within them. As we move toward multi-dimensionality, Space and Time are breaking apart. It will soon be the end of Time as we have known it. As a result, many people are starting to realize that we've been attracting things to ourselves since Time began.

There is No Spoon

> **There is energy connected with Thought...
> Thought can be pulsed and the energy
> connected with it becomes coherent
> and has a Laser-like Power.**
> **Dr. Marcel Vogel**

The beginning of the normal sleep pattern that humanity is about to experience will allow us to enter into enhanced states of creation. The magic of God's Universe is such that it was designed to provide us with the wonderful things in life. But we must send out what we want it to reflect back to us because the higher our consciousness is raised, the more the concept of Time breaks apart and the faster our thoughts are then manifested by the principle of attraction.

This new pattern of sleep is one in which we sleep for three hours, and then awaken in a higher dimensional state for two hours before returning to sleep. Because Time does not exist in the higher dimensions, the frequencies of the thoughts people hold in their minds during those two hours will quickly become their reality.

> **What we are today comes from our
> thoughts of yesterday, and our present
> thoughts build our life of tomorrow.
> Our Life is the creation of our Mind.**
> **Buddha Gautama**

As the weeks went by, I started to doubt whether Ken's business line would ever ring again and I began to worry about our financial situation. In the early morning hours, I had been experiencing this new pattern of sleep.

There is No Spoon

But now I was sending out the frequency of *Fear*, which was then being returned to me when I would awaken the following night, in much the same way in which a person is sent fear through a Voodoo doll that had been created in their likeness. I had fallen under the Law of Mind and there was very little Time to duck out of the way.

There is a lot of misguided information circulating about the future of mankind and, while actively searching for the truth of our reality, some of the spiritual literature I had read in the preceding weeks had also been manifesting as fear in me. So, by this time, I could no longer even pick up information that had a spiritual basis. The very act of touching a piece of spiritual literature was like putting my hand in a swamp only to feel the top of a crocodile's head beneath the surface of the water. Although my spiritual body had soared into a higher dimension, my emotional and physical bodies were struggling to catch up. It was an extremely terrifying time!

The job of our sub-conscious mind is to protect us. As a result, if we perceive something as bad, our sub-conscious will prepare our physical bodies to run away from it. This is the 'fight-or-flight' syndrome – a state that's required in order to flee from a predatory animal in the jungle. The overall effect of the stress hormones that are released cause several disturbing changes in the body. Ironically, it is this syndrome, itself, which we have learned to fear.

There is No Spoon

Unlike my sister, Lynn, whose initiation into spirituality was accomplished at a slow and steady pace, mine was a crash course of hard and fast lessons. She has lived her life like the tortoise in the story of *The Tortoise and the Hare*. In contrast, I am the hare. She would say to me, "You live life on the edge." And she was right. Aries people are 'doers,' not 'talkers'. That's why our lives are often filled with drama.

At the height of this particular drama, I said to Ken, *"I admit that I am powerless over fear."* Then I yelled at God, *"When will I get some peace and joy in MY LIFE? And NOT just fleeting moments of it!"*

That night, Don awoke from a dream in which he saw a vision of me drowning in a pool. What we are thinking and feeling at any time is no mystery to our guides and Angels. They can hear our thoughts because their sonic senses extend into the infrasonic and ultrasonic ranges. At some point in our evolutionary process, they will start coming to our aid as we begin to attract our own slow-moving darker energies back to ourselves during our 'dark night of the soul'. So, the following day, I was treated for the frequencies of *Anxiety*, *Fear*, *Paranoia* and *Self-Sabotage*.

Later, God sang to me the words from a Neil Diamond song. He sang, 'Stones would play inside her head, and where she slept they made her bed.' Initiation is an act of courage between the initiate and the divine. But it requires that we walk through some doors. Eventually, I was treated for the frequency of *Self-Destruction*.

> **I tell you the truth, until Heaven and**
> **Earth disappear, not the smallest letter,**
> **not the least stroke of a pen,**
> **will by any means disappear from the**
> **Law until everything is accomplished.**
> **Matthew 5:18**

One of the major shifts that we must make in order to reclaim the wisdom and power that the ancients have managed to hold onto is to move out from under the seven divine laws. We must begin instead to fulfill them.

The time has come for us to move into the power we have forgotten. But our Spirit won't allow us to do so until it knows it is safe. We must first clear the many, many emotions we have suppressed in our sub-conscious minds, and then learn to stop being a victim of them. To the degree that we are able to resonate with the higher vibrations, our lives will increasingly resonate with the higher dimensions. So we must learn to stay grounded.

> **I tell you the truth...**
> **before Abraham was born, I AM!**
> **John 8:58**

One night, God sang to me another Neil Diamond song. The song is called *I Am...I Said* and the part of the song I heard is sung, 'I Am, said I, and I am lost and can't even say why'. God had revealed to me that there is a special power behind the phrase 'I Am'.

Just as every thought produces a unique tone, so does every word produce a unique tone. So every word has its own unique frequency. But, if we state positive affirmations, such as 'I Am Peace,' 'I Am Love' and 'I Am Joy,' we can use the principle of attraction to transform negative thought forms. God gave this information to Moses when he saw the misery of the Israelites and heard them crying out to Him.

> **God said to Moses, "I AM that I AM.**
> **This is what you are to say to the Israelites:**
> **'I AM has sent me to you.'**
> **Exodus 3:14**

Eventually, I came to understand that emotions are just energies. Alone, they cannot harm us. It is what we perceive them to be that causes our bodies to engage with behavior mechanisms like the fight-or-flight syndrome.

The power of our sub-conscious mind can empower us or it can disempower us. We can run away from worry, grief or fear, but that only serves to feed it. We can keep ourselves distracted from it, or we can seek something external from ourselves as protection from it, but that only keeps it at bay. But if we claim the power behind it - the power of our sub-conscious mind - we can transform it.

One of the other five Platonic Solids is the Cube Octahedron, a powerful shape that provides for greater access to the part of us that exists outside Space and Time. Where the Star Tetrahedron is the electrical balance to magnetism, the Cube Octahedron is the magnetic balance to

There is No Spoon

electricity. During times of emotional stress, we can easily move through this super-conductive state if we visualize ourselves enveloped inside a Cube Octahedron that is made of Light. Visualizing in our minds the sacred geometries with which the true reality was created will help to return us to a state of balance.

In the final scene in the 1990s science-fiction movie *The Matrix*, the main character 'Neo' sees reality for what it really is, and then proceeds to stop bullets in mid-air. But he doesn't stop those bullets because he is able to resist them; he stops them because he no longer perceives them as part of his reality. He had become multi-dimensional.

By using visualization, we claim the enormous power of our sub-conscious mind. Neo was able to re-claim his power, and then use it to empower himself. There is neither good nor evil; there is only wisdom and ignorance. Life in this reality is simply a 'television screen' on which our beliefs play out as actions. So, when we change our beliefs, our sub-conscious mind changes 'the channel'. We need to move away from duality and out from under the seven divine laws. Nothing is bad; everything is just an experience.

This age is a time to eliminate all energies that no longer serve us. It is about finally understanding how to Lighten our load so we can attain the consciousness of the Christ. It is about walking the path that Jesus walked, as mature followers, with the capacity to finally understand how that is accomplished. We cannot walk the path to eternal life if we have fear in our hearts.

> **God did not give us a Spirit of timidity,**
> **but a Spirit of power, of love**
> **and of self-discipline.**
> II Timothy 1:7

It took seven months of persistent effort and the help of Don and my Angels to master the Law of Mind, to regain my self-confidence and to rid myself of unrelenting torment. And, throughout it all, I continued to play the role of Doubting Thomas.

But, when the nightmare was over, my Angels gave me a special mandala to help me evolve beyond the chatter of my busy mind. Mandalas have both spiritual and ritual significance in Buddhism and Hinduism. In meditation, they can help us to listen with a subdued ego and encourage extra-sensory perception by breaking down barriers between our Spirit and our conscious and sub-conscious minds. Where prayer allows us to talk to God, meditation allows God to reply. The mandala I was given was carved from Mother of Pearl, in the shape of the flower of the Lotus.

> **It is already complete in the ethers.**
> **We're just going through the motions**
> **in the physical realm.**
> Dr. Leonard G. Horowitz, DMD

In the same way that we resonate with everyone and everything around us, we also resonate with our Earth. And, at this time in history, the frequency of the Earth is rising exponentially. It will soon reach 13 Hz, the frequency on which the Mayan Tzolk'in calendar is based - the frequency of *Unconditional Love*.

As we move toward 2012, we will be evolving back into our core personality where we will find a confidence in who we truly are. Our core personality is not hampered by human thought patterns and belief systems.

But a key component of our evolution will be our willingness and ability to adapt to the Earth's higher alpha waves. Whether people are aware of it or not, our energetic systems are being affected by this increasing frequency, both from a physiological and a geophysical standpoint. So we will need to dispel any beliefs and behaviors that don't fit into the new paradigm.

> **So you also must be ready,**
> **because the Son of Man will come at**
> **an hour when you do not expect him.**
> **Matthew 24:44**

All of humanity is rapidly becoming multi-dimensional. We will soon be living in a world shaped by our feelings and expectations, rather than by our physical efforts. Space and Time are illusions of the third and fourth dimensions. Our future self exists beyond Time and Space. It is the self that lives in a multi-dimensional reality. So we will soon be able to exist anywhere at any Time.

There is No Spoon

> **We are on the brink of possibilities
> that will make us literally unrecognizable
> to ourselves... not in the next thousand
> years but in the next 20 years.**
> Terence McKenna

When we reach this state, there will be no delay between our causes and the effects. We will achieve simply through the process of thought. We will have total control over matter solely with our minds. Our thought forms, themselves, will become the manifestation. It is we who are responsible for making Heaven on Earth a reality.

> **Is it not written in your law
> I have said You are Gods?**
> John 10:34

God gave us the power to create our own reality. And, solely with our own minds, we have set into motion a game of Creation for ourselves. Our holographic reality is nothing more than a dream from which we are all starting to awaken - a gigantic network of akashic energy from which everyone accesses the same data, simultaneously and in real-time. And God is the dreamer.

> **Nothing we perceive as material and
> real exists, other than as a dream
> that we're projecting onto the world.**
> Dr. Alberto Villoldo, PhD

The coding for the entire universe is stored in binary format in our DNA. The holographic memory of the human genome enables our DNA bio-computer to form images of bio-structures, holographically. Our reality is nothing more than particle-waves, like the binary computer readouts that are conceptualized in the movie *The Matrix*.

> **We must assume behind this force
> the existence of a conscious and
> intelligent mind. This mind is
> the Matrix of Matter.**
> Dr. Max Planck, PhD

This 'game of Life' is, by far, the biggest, most spectacular game of virtual reality we will ever play. In this game, the future never arrives and the present moves at the speed of thought into a past that is simply a collection of electro-magnetic imprints called *memories*.

> **You will know the truth,
> and the truth will set you free.**
> John 8:32

But this virtual reality is about to end, having come full circle in the cycles of Time. So it is the people who have the mental attitude that provides for success by way of conscious prayer who will manifest the changes in our new world. There is no spoon...

The Lightworker

In the first age of humanity's evolution as cave dwellers, we worshipped through fear because it was all we could understand. In the *Book of Exodus*, which is part of the Torah, it is written that God inflicted ten plagues upon the Egyptians before they finally released their Hebrew slaves, the final plague being the killing of all firstborn sons. It is also written that God instructed the Hebrews to mark their doors with the blood of a lamb so He would pass over their homes and spare their sons. In remembrance of God's promise, the Jewish people celebrate this event as a holy day they call Passover.

In the Gospels of the New Testament, it is written that the Eucharist was the final meal Jesus shared with his disciples before his arrest and crucifixion two-thousand years ago. It was during his last supper that he announced the coming of this shift of the ages. And the planetary cycles support his prophecy.

> **When will this happen, and what will be the sign of Your coming and of the End of the Age?**
> Matthew 24:3

The transition from one astrological age to another happens every 2160 years, the last being from the age of Aries to the age of Pisces. The zodiac sign of Aries isn't an adult Ram. It is the Passover Lamb. And that age culminated with the arrival of Jesus, the first arrival of Christ consciousness.

> **God will bring with Jesus those who
> have fallen Asleep in him.**
> I Thessalonians 4:14

Astrological systems typically divide the horoscope into twelve 'houses,' the positions of which depend on Space and Time, rather than on a date on a calendar. Each sign of the astrological zodiac starts its house at the intersection with the previous sign. So, as we leave the age of Pisces, the sinners and the saints, we enter the eleventh house – the age of Aquarius, whose zodiacal sign is the Water Bearer, the Holy Spirit.

> **As you enter the City, a Man carrying a
> Jar of Water will meet you. Follow him to the
> House that he Enters... He will show you a
> large Upper Room, all furnished.**
> Luke 22:8-10

Ascended masters are spiritually enlightened people who, during the course of many lifetimes of devotion to God, have fulfilled their mission, as Jesus did, and have perfected the process of yoga and ascended back to God. They are a large group of Western saints and Eastern masters who are united in a Great White Brotherhood.

Those of us who have incarnated at this time chose to do so to experience that same personal ascension and to witness planetary ascension to a higher vibratory, multi-dimensional state. We have chosen to sacrifice an entire

The Lightworker

lifetime to serve in the upliftment of mankind. But this is not without its rewards. Such service results in great spiritual growth.

Jesus and the Great White Brotherhood have chosen to remain connected with us, in order to guide us down the path to our own self-realization. They are directing the spiritual evolution of those of us who desire to reunite with God. We have a direct line to any of them through our own ability to enter the divine.

In this age, our test will be the acceptance of our healing and our patience with it. If we pass this simple test, we will be worthy of the higher realms of consciousness, which will then flow into us during our mission here. We will then gain the authority to pass healing on to others. Only through experience of one's own healing will a person gain this authority.

One evening, I asked my Angels, *"Why am I here?"* They replied, *"You came here to heal; first to heal yourself, and then to heal the many others who will also be awakening to the Truth."* It was at this point in my evolution that I realized my role as a Lightworker - one who sends out Light in order to lead the way for others.

**You are the Light of the world.
A City on a hill cannot be hidden.**
Matthew 5:14

The Lightworker

The Lightworker is almost always a solitary person who does not fit into fixed structures of society. They are naturally anti-authoritarian and feel drawn to becoming therapists or teachers. They deeply honor and respect life, which often manifests as a fondness for plants and animals, and a concern for the environment. The destruction of parts of these kingdoms on the Earth invokes in them deep feelings of loss and grief.

The soul of the Lightworker is older than most other souls on the Earth. They have lived many lives preparing for this age, sometimes deeply involved in spirituality, incarnating as monks, nuns, hermits, psychics and shamans. For fulfilling these roles, they were often rejected and persecuted, the traumas from which have left deep scars within them.

> **Only those who have obtained
> illumination through union with the Light
> which dwells in the hearts of all
> can became the Light of the world.**
> Swami Prabhavananda

One of the factors blocking their self-realization is that they carry a heavy karmic burden, which can lead them astray for a long time. But, when they make their way through this burden and release the need for power, they realize that they are beings of Light.

Once it begins, the Lightworker has the capacity for a rapid spiritual awakening. If they choose it, they can move down that path faster than most other people, which enables

The Lightworker

them to bring others along with them. But first, they must go through the process themselves. This generally demands great determination and perseverance. When they start this journey, all of their lifetimes come to the surface, leaving them in states of self-doubt and hopelessness.

> **Do not harm the land or the sea or the trees until we put a seal on the Foreheads of the servants of our God.**
> **Revelation 7:3**

While on their journey toward enlightenment, the Lightworker sends a Light to guide other souls into 'safe harbors'. Because they are strong and solidly built, only a few Lightworkers are needed to affect many other 'seafaring souls'. By the Law of Vibration, they literally change the frequency of the planet wherever they walk. As each Lightworker holds the Light, the frequencies of other souls are being affected and changed.

It requires only one-half of one percent of the people in the world to awaken to the truth in order to make a profound shift in the collective consciousness. Inevitably, as more and more people awaken, the Earth will succumb to the Light. When it does, the world will catapult into multi-dimensionality and we will be able to perceive of that which has been around us all along. In this age, we will see the second coming of the mind of Christ.

> **His Name will be on their Foreheads.**
> **Revelation 22:4**

The Lightworker

Something very few people in this generation will do is to retrieve all of the spiritual knowledge they have ever learned from all of their lifetimes on the Earth. Within our akashic field is stored a metaphoric spiritual 'jar of knowledge'. With each life we live, this jar fills up with the truths that we learn about life and the Universe. When we reincarnate, it is still filled to the same level it was at when we lived our previous life. Most people never open that jar. But, if they do, mastery is within their reach.

One evening, I told Don I wanted to open that jar. So my Angels retrieved from my DNA what they referred to as 'one dropper-full from an ocean of information'. Then, they said, *"You will have to earn the remainder of that ocean. Everything we do from this point on will have to be done out of Love"*.

We then retrieved from my akash a consciousness I had previously held as an ancient monk named JIHAAD. This was a life I had lived long before the time of Christ or Buddha, a life I had lived as a member of a brotherhood, one that was devoted to a discipline prescribed by a spiritual order. The process of retrieving the consciousness of this former self was like downloading the Sparring program to the character of 'Neo' in *The Matrix*.

There are six quantum energies that are involved in the gifts of this age. These involve the twelve layers of our DNA, which we can activate to a point where great gifts are ours if we choose them. Some of our DNA layers have been lying dormant for thousands of years, waiting to be activated when the Earth's energy reaches the frequency at which it is currently vibrating. This activation isn't apparent in our physical structure. It is in our chemistry.

In the multi-dimensional horserace that your order of spiritual guidance is watching, the horse that is currently winning the race is the life you are most likely to live in the perceived future. And, although that horse carries with it the most probable outcome, the outcome can be changed. Your DNA is a Time machine.

With each subsequent appointment, Don and I continued performing similar processes, which my Angels referred to as 'unwrapping'. They would repeatedly refer to it as the removal of 'the veil', the illusion of duality. The Greek word *Apokálypsis* means 'lifting of the veil,' a term applied to the disclosure to certain privileged persons of something hidden from the majority of mankind.

> **I saw the Holy City, the new Jerusalem,
> coming down out of heaven from God,
> prepared as a Bride...**
> **Revelation 21:2**

The third initiation that must be performed to attain the mind of the Christ requires a level of mastery over the mental body. This is the level at which we learn to control our thoughts. At this level, we don't merely push away unwanted thought waves, but rather, our mind is transformed and our perspectives are shifted.

The Lightworker

At this level in my spiritual awareness, I have come to understand that the events that cause our emotional issues are deliberately orchestrated by our Spirit. This is done for our own growth and for the growth of humanity.

The people who cause your issues are not really responsible for their actions at all. It is their compassionate Spirit who, from a higher realm, agrees for them to play the bad guys in each of the dramas in your life. And your Spirit also agrees for you to play the bad guy from time to time, so they too can grow spiritually. Both of these Spirits, yours and theirs, love you more than you could ever know from your current perspective.

The minute we release the grudges we have held toward others for playing their part in our dramas, our subconscious mind informs our Spirit that these grudges no longer have a hold on us. That's when our Spirit opens for us a direct line of communication with God.

> **Whenever anyone turns to the Lord,**
> **the Veil is taken away.**
> II Corinthians 3:16

Later, my Angels suggested I take the essence of the Dorothy Wycoff Pieris flower. The definition for this essence is 'For the completion and the resolution; for the finishing of the issue that has been hanging around for a long time. To help shift the energy of the person into a state where they naturally release the old state of being and move on, so that the old issues are no more than a distant memory - a faint echo of a distant past, barely remembered.'

Now I no longer perceive Jesus as some mystical being from within the clouds. Instead, I understand him to be Jesus, our brother. And I understand myself to be Shahalah, his sister and friend. I understand how he would have volunteered to incarnate in human form, at a time when people were still incapable of fully understanding what they needed to know in order to follow him back to the higher realms. He understood he would forget his divinity and that he would have to find it again through his own works. He knew what he would endure in this process, but he volunteered in spite of this simply because it had to be done.

> **Why would a drop of water serve itself**
> **instead of the cosmic ocean**
> **of which it is a part?**
> Dr. Joshua David Stone, PhD

The heart of the Christ embraces humanity with compassion but without judgment. That heart recognizes all experiences in this world as those it has gone through itself. That heart has lived the role of the aggressor and that of the sufferer; the role of the master and of the slave. When the Christ in me watches a conflict between people or nations, now I try not to judge.

> **In the last days, said God,**
> **I will Pour out my Spirit upon all flesh.**
> Acts 2:17

At my next appointment with Don, my Angels suggested to me the essence of the Alexander Rose. The definition for this essence is 'To know the real God-Self within; to come into a full experiential understanding of my friendship with God; to trust God in everything; to love God unconditionally as God loves us; to embrace God as God embraces us; to use God for everything in our lives; to help God as God helps us; to thank God, knowing that everything we need is already provided, even before we ask'. This essence was given to me to help smooth the way for my winning horse on its journey home ...

Deceptions en Masse

Soon after the crucifixion of Jesus the Christ, a Greek religious movement began in the areas around Greece, Egypt and Israel. In 42 AD, Saint Mark the Apostle established the Coptic Orthodox Church and the Catechetical School in Alexandria, Egypt. At that time, a large number of people embraced the Christian faith and Christianity began to spread throughout Egypt.[46]

The first Christians in Egypt were mainly Alexandrian Jews who adopted the cross as the symbol for Christianity. Ideas from the Greek movement then merged with those of early Christianity to form a philosophy called Christian Gnosticism.

In 70 AD, in what was to be the first of three wars between the Jews and the Romans, the Roman army conquered and massacred a large portion of the Jewish population.[47] Jesus' followers managed to survive 300 years of persecution under the Roman Empire before they were finally eradicated.

Dr. Elaine Pagels is the Harrington Spear Paine Professor of Religion at Princeton University. In her book, *The Gnostic Gospels*, she writes that, by the second century AD, the Catholic Church of Rome had declared itself to be the authority on religious teachings.[48]

Deceptions en Masse

At that time, Saint Irenæus was an early Catholic Church Father. He was the author of five works titled *The Destruction and Overthrow of Falsely So-Called Knowledge*. He wrote them in an attempt to overthrow those who were writing about the process of reincarnation and all the other philosophies he considered to be heresy. Saint Irenæus was the Bishop of Lugdunum, in Gaul, which was part of Rome. As a result, his writings were formative in the early development of Christian theology.

In 364 AD, in an event known as the Council of Laodicea, the early Roman Church Fathers made a decision as to which of the Greek and Hebrew texts would be included in the Holy Bible. When Emperor Constantine made Christianity the official religion of Rome, the possession of the books Bishop Irenæus had declared to be heretical was made a criminal offence. Copies of them were then burned and destroyed.

Shortly thereafter, the truths that had been taught by the Greeks and the Egyptians were dismissed as mythology. As a result, Jesus' secret teachings were literally driven underground and our wisdom was lost from the collective consciousness.

The Church of Rome refused to allow the Bible to be available in any language other than Latin. Subsequently, all of the Greek and Hebrew texts they included were translated into Latin. At that time, few people, other than Catholic priests, could read Latin. So it was then that we

Deceptions en Masse

became accustomed to giving away our power to people who undertook to dialog with God on our behalf.

> **Even if our Gospel is Veiled, it is**
> **Veiled to those who are perishing.**
> II Corinthians 4:2-3

In the year 882 AD, some Jews who were living in Egypt bought and renovated a Coptic church, and then turned it into the Ben Ezra Synagogue. At that time, it was the custom for worn out books, which were written in the Hebrew language, to be stored in the synagogue, in a special archive, or genizah. One-thousand years later, this archive was discovered to contain hundreds of thousands of forgotten texts. This collection, which has come to be known as the Cairo Genizah, comprises the largest and most diverse collection of medieval manuscripts in the entire world.[49]

Around the time of the discovery of these texts, archaeologists who were digging in Upper Egypt found a few fragments of a text that was even older than those that were found in the synagogue. It was written on papyrus, which are flattened stalks of a reed that grows in the Nile River Valley. This ancient text was titled *Gospel of Thomas*.[50]

Shortly thereafter, the teenaged sons of an Arab peasant rode out to a cliff to dig for fertilizer, near a town in Upper Egypt called Nag Hammadi. While he was digging, one of the boys hit a large clay jar that held thirteen ancient leather-bound books. When they were sold illegally through antiquities dealers, twelve of the books were confiscated by the Egyptian government and deposited in the Coptic Museum in Cairo. The thirteenth book was smuggled out of Egypt and purchased by the Jung Foundation in Switzerland.[51]

These books contain translations of ancient manuscripts, one of which corresponds to the papyrus fragment of the *Gospel of Thomas*. Along with a text titled *Gospel of Philip*, they are collectively referred to as the Gnostic Gospels.

Since the discovery of these gospels, other ancient scrolls have been found concealed in caves near the ruins of an old settlement, called the Qumran, on the northwestern shore of the Dead Sea. Known as the Dead Sea Scrolls, these scrolls consist of roughly 900 texts.[52]

Twenty-five percent of the Dead Sea Scrolls is biblical scripture that includes some of the only known copies of first-century biblical documents. With the exception of the book of *Esther*, every single book of the Old Testament was discovered there. But what is most interesting is that the book of *Esther* is the only book that does not make reference to God.

> **The mystery that has been kept hidden for ages and generations, but is now disclosed to the Saints.**
> **Colossians 1:25-26**

Deceptions en Masse

The Old Testament originally contained a collection of over one dozen texts called the Apocrypha. Derived from the Greek word *apocryphal*, it means 'things that are hidden'. King James of England imposed heavy fines on anyone who printed the Old Testament without including the Apocrypha. So it was included in the original King James version of the Bible, which was printed in the year 1611.[53] But 250 years later, the Archbishop of Canterbury officially removed it from that version.[54]

The *Book of Ben Sira*, a volume of wise proverbs that was discovered in the Ben Ezra Synagogue, is part of these apocryphal texts. Known also as the *Book of Wisdom* and as *The Wisdom of Jesus son of Sirach*, this book was originally written in Hebrew in the second century BC. Eventually, it was included in the Old Testament as the book of *Ecclesiastes*. Before its discovery, no known Hebrew version existed. Some scholars even doubted its existence.

The *Book of Enoch* is also part of the apocryphal texts. This ancient book describes an age in which Heaven will exist on the Earth. It is interesting to note that the books of *Jude* and *Hebrews*, which have both been retained in the Bible, actually quote directly from the *Book of Enoch*, which has not. In fact, there are over twenty books that are referred to in the Bible, but that have been excluded from it.

Many Christians believe that God would never have allowed his Word to be tampered with in ways he didn't want. And, they are absolutely correct. But, it must be

Deceptions en Masse

understood that God has allowed this cover-up to take place. If we had known these truths two-thousand years ago, we would have distorted them out of our own ignorance to such an extent that, now, when we need them the most, we wouldn't be able to recognize them for what they truly are.

> **Brothers, I could not address you as spiritual but as worldly - mere infants in Christ. I gave you milk, not solid food, for you were not yet ready for it.**
> I Corinthians 3:1-2

There are over 900 versions of the Holy Bible in circulation today. The Bible of the Jewish people consists of just 24 books, whereas there are 66 books for Protestants, 73 for Catholics and 78 for most Orthodox Christians. And it isn't difficult to see the many, many discrepancies that exist between them, some of which profoundly affect religious doctrine.

As an example, in today's King James version, chapter 13 of the *Book of Revelation* begins 'And I stood upon the sand of the sea,' whereas in the New International version, it begins 'And the dragon stood on the shore of the sea'. It is also written in that same book that, if anyone adds to or removes from its words, God will take away their share in the Tree of Life. But, obviously, that threat didn't stop people from doing so.

The hymns that were originally given to the Church of Rome were intended to be heart-felt music for our spiritual evolution. The tone of Ut in the Solfeggio musical scale prepares our consciousness to receive the other tones in the scale. But, at some point in history, it was replaced with the tone of Do. This significantly decreased the effectiveness of the scale as a whole, which now consists of the tones Do, Re, Mi, Fa, Sol, La.

The frequencies of the tones Re, Mi, Fa and Sol are also for the commencement of the overlay of the DNA construct, to repair any damaged DNA strands, to help us return to our original DNA blueprint and to reconnect the remainder of our twelve DNA strands.[55]

It is pure sounds that bring the right hemisphere of the brain online. When sound is articulated from a high level of understanding, it can cause energy to be demoted down to matter and it can also cause matter to be promoted back to energy. When sung in sequential harmony, the tones in the original Solfeggio scale vibrate at the exact frequencies required to open our cells so new programming can be imprinted on our DNA. The final tone in the scale, that of La, is for returning to spiritual order. In other words, the scale was designed to elevate matter to Spirit.

God always takes the simplest way.
Albert Einstein

In Lima, Peru, the Office for the Extirpation of Idolatries is still in operation today, after having been established 500 years ago. The Church of Rome considers the ancient spiritual wisdom of the Maya, Hopi, Laika and Inca people to be so threatening that it continues to maintain the operation of this office, the purpose of which is still to eradicate their religious practices.[56]

When Dr. Alberto Villoldo left his work as a psychologist to enter the Andes Mountains of Peru, he was taken under the wing of one of the last of these Laika, a University Professor by day and a master shaman by night. Dr. Villoldo once told him that he felt lucky to have found him, to which the shaman replied, "If the Church hasn't found us in the last 500 years, what makes you think YOU found ME?"

> **Men ought to regard us as servants of Christ and as those entrusted with the secret things of God.**
> 1 Corinthians 4:1

In 396 AD, a Roman Catholic priest was named the Bishop of Hippo Regius, a title he held for thirty-four years. Also known as Saint Augustine, he is perhaps the most prolific writer of the Middle Ages, having written an estimated five or six million words. In 428 AD, at the end of his life, he wrote a document in Latin, titled *Retractationes*, the English translation of which means 'to retreat from'. The purpose of this document was to note, in chronological order, those passages from all his previous works in which he had either made an error or later changed his viewpoint. In one of the chronological entries in this document is written the following:[57]

Deceptions en Masse

> **That which is called the Christian religion existed among the Ancients, and never did not exist, from the beginning of the Human race until Christ came in the flesh, at which time the true religion, which already existed, began to be called Christianity.'**
>
> St. Augustine

In 1967, a Professor of Theology, named Dr. Miceál Ledwith, became a Roman Catholic priest at the Wexford Ireland Diocese of Ferns. He then became a member of the distinguished International Theological Commission, which was set up by the Vatican in Rome to advise the Pope on theological matters. Eventually, he rose to become advisor to Pope John Paul II, himself. But, after thirty years, he left the orders to become a teacher at a school of ancient wisdom in Washington because of what he has come to believe is the real truth of the story of Jesus Christ and his teachings, and of the truth of our existence.[58]

> **Some have gone so far as to say that it will shake the foundation of conventional Christianity.**
>
> Dr. Miceál Ledwith

The goal of Jesus' followers, the Christian Gnostics, was to make the reasoning mind an instrument of our spiritual nature. Just as the word *agnostic* means 'without wisdom,' the word *gnostic* means 'with wisdom'. And, in the *Gospel of Thomas,* the opening lines read, 'These are the secret words which the living Jesus spoke, and which his brother, Judas Thomas, wrote down'.

Deceptions en Masse

> **Gnosticism is about to become the
> 21st century world religion.**
> **Prof. Gilles Quispel**

Gnostics didn't look to salvation from sin, but rather, from the ignorance of which sin is a consequence. When the texts in the Old Testament were eventually translated into English, the Greek word *metanoia* was translated as 'repentance'. However, this word actually signifies much more than simply asking for forgiveness of sins. It literally means 'to change your mind'. Furthermore, the word *hamartia* was translated as 'to sin'. But the word actually originated with the sport of archery. It means 'to miss the mark'.

> **Do not conform any longer to the pattern of
> this world, but be transformed by
> the Renewing of your Mind.**
> **Romans 12:2**

The second coming of Christ is the raising of the consciousness of all of humanity to his level. So, as we make an effort to 'change our minds,' it is expected that, occasionally, we will 'miss the mark'.

> **Then I looked, and there before me was
> the Lamb... and with him 144,000 who had
> his Name and his Father's Name
> written on their Foreheads.**
> **Revelation 14:1**

God has been watching us, guiding us and preparing us for this change of mind for thousands of years. Now that

Deceptions en Masse

we are finally ready for this higher level information, we are being led to discover it.

> **Multitudes who Sleep in the dust
> of the Earth will Awake.**
> **Daniel 12:2**

We have been ignorant about the truth of our existence. And we have been ignorant about the existence of intelligent beings, who live in peace and love within our solar system, and of the important role they are playing in the unfolding of God's divine plan. But, at this time in history, the veil is being pulled away from the entire planet. A critical mass is about to be reached in the area of world truth.

> **The hardest thing to explain
> is the glaringly evident which
> everybody had decided not to see.**
> **Ayn Rand**

And when the Mayan god Quetzalcoatl returns to Earth from out of the current galactic alignment, it will be us who carry the mind of Christ into the next age...

The Fall

There is an underlying force that allows for Creation. One part of the force attracts, like a magnet pulling toward another. The other part repels. The magnet itself is neutral. So God, like a magnet, creates both forces, but is Himself neutral.

It was through the joys of creativity and in the sharing of it that God desired to separate Himself into smaller and smaller fragments. So, in the Outbreath of God, seven Spirits stood before Him. These Spirits then divided themselves down through the various levels to that of individual souls. With each split, the fragments lowered in frequency. We are all children of God and, as part of God, we are God.

> **Now if we are Children, then we are heirs—
> heirs of God and co-heirs with Christ.**
> **Romans 8: 17**

The seven Spirits then set off to create the Universe with colors of Light, using frequencies that are formed on 144,000 revolutions per millisecond. They used the Torah as a blueprint for the work of creating the Universe. The letters in the Hebrew alphabet were used in pre-determined combinations to accomplish this task. Its origin was a Creation that uses the laws of substance - of physics.

The primary forces emanating from the black hole at the centre of the galaxy include gravity and repulsion, which bends and captures Light. So the black hole became responsible for expansion and contraction in the Universe. We all watched in angelic form as the repelling force pushed the matter apart and the attracting force, which was expressed as the force of gravity, collected that matter into stars and planets. Creation cannot happen without the repelling force being the dominant force.

Every planet was set to vibrate at a different frequency, playing a different musical tone within the Music of the Spheres. The Universe was united in song – in verse.

> **He chose us in Him before
> the Creation of the world.**
> **Ephesians 1:4**

As immortal souls, we then entered into incarnation in the physical form, each with eleven lives to experience. Our challenging game began in a grand Polynesian garden that floated continuously on the face of the water. We lived in colors of Light, free of matter and completely infused with Spirit, in peace with ourselves and in harmony with the forces of nature - in a land we called Lemuria.

> **So God created Man in his own image,
> in the image of God he created him.**
> **Genesis 1:27**

While incarnate as Man in this game of Life, we were able to experience sensation, something pure consciousness cannot do. We were able to embrace all of the physical,

The Fall

mental and emotional stimuli that Man can experience, everything that life has to offer.

When a new game began, we established a land called Atlantis. Eventually, we learned to build pyramids with which to transmit energy using quartz Crystals. It was through telepathy that we programmed these Crystals. One pyramid intensified and transmitted energies to the others, which would then act as receiving devices. These devices would disperse energy as it was needed.

But, at some point, one of the seven Spirits took it upon itself to experiment with the frequency of the color black. This created the Law of Polarity, without which we would have no choices in Life. This law allowed us the freedom to choose, or 'free will'. We who participated in this experiment were one-third of all the angels in Heaven. We felt that Man couldn't truly understand love and joy, without experiencing loss and despair.

The mixing of black with colors of a lighter variety produced as many shades of grey as there are shades of Light. So we went through Life simply choosing between them. But the cellular structures of the human being cannot hold the darker frequencies. They were meant to be infused with Light. So, when this 'forbidden fruit' was eaten, Man came to perceive of the polarities of good and evil.

> **Behold, the Man has become like one of us, to know good and evil.**
> **Genesis 3:22**

The Fall

Because of the dark frequencies that had been infused into the cells of our incarnated selves, the left hemisphere of our brains became more dominant and our bodies of Light became heavy and dense.

> **The LORD God made garments of skin for Adam...**
> **Genesis 3:22**

Out of curiosity, Man gradually became attached to the things in Life. And, out of pride, he began to think that the original Creation could be improved upon. As a result, some of the things he created had a devastating effect on the Earth, which now wobbles like a top in its orbit around the Sun, on an angle that is not sacred geometry. This wobble changed its frequency, flattening its musical tone.

In these games of Life, as long as the energies maintain their equilibrium, the Universe remains undifferentiated. But, by the end of the last cycle 13,000 years ago, much of humanity had lost its spirituality. Our Light had grown dim. And by greatly disturbing the delicate balance of nature, a re-creation of the Universe began.

> **What harmony is there between Christ and Belial?**
> **2 Corinthians 6:15**

In this re-creation process, the North and South poles reversed themselves, which caused the melting of the polar icecaps and the beginning of the Ice Age. This meltdown eventually caused the great continents of Lemuria and

The Fall

Atlantis to sink to the ocean floor in an event that claimed the lives of 64 million people. This catastrophe brought about the end of the world as we knew it and left a field of electro-magnetic energy in an area of the sea now known as the Bermuda Triangle.

> **Though by this time you ought to be teachers,**
> **you need someone to teach you the elementary**
> **truths of God's Word all over again.**
> **Hebrews 5:11-12**

In spite of this fall of humanity, an Atlantean priest managed to retain his spirituality and remain close to God. And, while the rest of humanity lost its immortality, he and a few other members of the priesthood migrated to Khemit, the area now known as Egypt. It is because of the shifting of the poles that Lower Egypt is geographically located above Upper Egypt and the Nile River flows upstream.

There is only one God and one true reality. But there are many, many ways in which we can perceive it. So these few immortal masters set in place a plan to slowly guide Man back to the levels of Christ consciousness from which he had descended. This grand plan included a new reality called Zep Tepi, or Genesis.

It was the Atlantean who was the recorder and balancer of the words that created our current reality. His intention kept the forces in Heaven and Earth in equilibrium. He based the blueprint of this reality on the mathematics of sacred geometry. It was his skill in celestial mathematics that made proper use of the laws upon which the foundation of the Universe rests.

> **In the beginning was the Word,**
> **and the Word was with God,**
> **and the Word was God.**
>
> John 1:1

In an effort to regain control of Life on the Earth, our spiritual selves decided that, when we incarnate into this world, we will forget our true nature and the knowledge of everything in the Universe. It takes wisdom to use knowledge, something we can only attain through experience. So we placed a gap between the two hemispheres of our brains to completely obliterate the memories of who we truly are. It was better to live with the limitations of the third dimension than to risk misusing our divine powers within it. The Time matrix was added as an external framework, in order to reduce the speed at which our thoughts become reality.

This choice was necessary to the development of mankind. It gave us the opportunity to evolve in consciousness so we would be ready to advance to the next level of spirituality by the end of the current 26,000 year cycle. Those of us who made this choice fell under the seven divine laws and readily submitted ourselves to being played as pawns in this game. When the karmic wheel of reincarnation began to turn, we became trapped by ignorance in this illusion. And where there is pleasure, there is also pain.

The Fall

> **The mind is its own place, and in itself can make a Heaven of Hell, a Hell of Heaven.**
>
> John Milton

Beneath the Giza plateau in Egypt, the Atlantean and the other masters developed a network of tunnels. In a Hall of Records, they carved out our true history in hieroglyphics, which they knew would be decipherable by today's linguistics. Then they encoded the knowledge of the higher spiritual dimensions using the languages of mathematics, geometry and astronomy so it would be discovered in this millennium by those of us who could decipher it.

They buried this information deep beneath a great lioness who would await the time when our consciousness would reach a level at which we could decipher how the music of Creation was written. Everything they constructed was harmonically tuned to specific frequencies and musical sequences that, when 'played,' will open the Hall of Records.

On top of the plateau, they built great stone pyramids to act as voice-activated geophysical computers. They designed the Great Pyramid as both an initiation chamber and as a Time capsule. It maintains the illusion of Time by way of the Precession of the Equinoxes.

When it was constructed around 10,450 BC, the Great Pyramid was erected in the exact center of the land mass of Earth. Its height corresponds to the radius of a circle; the circumference of its base correlates to the

The Fall

perimeter of a sphere. These proportions were chosen because they are in resonance with the universal principals of the movement of energy and the Creation of matter.

There were over two million stone blocks used in the construction of the Great Pyramid, some of which weigh as much as 40 tons. The masters used telepathy to move these stones into place. High-frequency, ultra-violet sound waves were used to electro-magnetically fuse the massive blocks of stone together. It had a layered capstone that served as a conductor of solar energy, which was collected through Crystals in the apex of the structure. White marble casing stones formed its smooth outer surface. The masters called this grand structure *The Light*.

Along the west side of the Nile River, they built twelve temples, which they used as schools of higher wisdom. Inside the temples they performed initiations to prepare initiates for their ascension back to the higher dimensions. Because pyramids amplify whatever energy lies beneath them, the final initiation and rites took place inside the Great Pyramid.

It was decided that, at the beginning of every age, seven great sages would meet to evaluate the state of our evolution. These seven sages include Meng-ste from China, Vidyapati from India, Kaspar from Persia, Ashbina from Assyria, Apollo from Greece, Matheno from Egypt and Philo from Israel. They determine how far toward justice, love and righteousness humanity has come. They formulate the

The Fall

code of laws, religious postulates and the plans of rule that are best suited to the coming age.

> **Remember the height
> from which you have fallen.**
> **Revelation 2:5**

Over time, a small agricultural community established itself around the Mediterranean Sea. Ignorant of the fact that they were living under the seven divine laws, they unconsciously created a virtual reality out of which grew the civilization of ancient Rome. And, because we were all spiritually asleep in a descending age, this Roman civilization eventually came to dominate, through conquest and assimilation, those of us who were living in Western Europe and the Mediterranean region.

Around 2000 BC, it was decided that a soul should incarnate into this illusion, with the purpose of becoming the father of a race – a man so devoted to God that he would be called A-Brahm. It was hoped that, through him, humanity would eventually demonstrate that it could be trusted with the divine powers it possesses.

A-Brahm settled in the land of Canaan, near the southeastern shore of the Mediterranean Sea. When his grandson fathered twelve sons who established settlements on the west bank of the Jordan River, A-Brahm became the father of the Hebrew race. The mountains there became the core of the region that was settled by these twelve Hebrew tribes.

The Fall

In about 1000 BC, a man named David was born into the tribe of Judah. When the rest of the community elected him to rule over them, he conquered the neighboring settlement of Jerusalem, which had initially been allocated to the tribe of Benjamin. He then made it the capital of the United Kingdom of Israel. The Israelites there practiced the religion of Judaism and came to be known as Jews.

The Atlantean priest was known to the Egyptian people as Thoth. He was depicted in their glyphs with the head of an ibis. Because of his wisdom, the people worshipped Thoth and the other immortal masters as deities, viewing them as the pilots of Space vehicles. The masters tried to teach the people mastery, but the people wanted only to worship them. So, eventually, it was decided that we, the people of the world, needed to develop without their guidance.

At that time, Thoth transformed himself into a Greek and called himself Hermes Trismegistus. Then he began to teach the sciences of mathematics and geometry to Pythagoras, the Greek philosopher. All of the fundamental wisdom that is embedded in the teachings of every race of Man can be traced back to the teachings of the immortal Hermes. It was he who established the three universal principles of alchemy, astrology and psychology. His knowledge promulgated through the writing of over 20,000 books, which became the basis of the oldest cultures and religions today.

The Fall

Over time, the Egyptian dynasty began to decline and most of the temples were destroyed by war. But Pythagoras, the philosopher, founded a religious movement called Pythagoreanism. The Greek culture flourished because of his Pythagorean Italic School, eventually becoming much larger than the area of modern day Greece.

The wisdom of the Egyptians also moved into the Jewish culture in Israel. But, in 536 BC, the Jews were conquered by the King of Persia, who lived in what is now southern Iran. At that time, the Persian empire was much vaster than modern day Iran. The Jews became influenced by Persian religion, which taught them the concepts of reward and punishment, Heaven and Hell, and the Judgment Day. So it was decided that the oversoul of A-Brahm would incarnate as a Messiah, in an effort to make a more powerful impetus for change in the world.

This same oversoul had already previously fragmented itself into many different souls, in many different times and places, including that of the Atlantean priest. He was the avatar who had founded the many different world religions.

Around 500 BC, several of the masters incarnated in Israel and formed a community called the Essene Brotherhood, a co-ed monastic community that was located in and around the city of Jerusalem. Their sole purpose was to prepare the way for the coming of the Messiah into the world.

The Fall

In 186 BC, the Essene's spread into a community called the Qumran. It was from this community that a mortal named Jeshua ben Joseph was born, the Jewish child who would grow into the man we know as Jesus. Through his birth was brought an elevated energy. He was infused with the Light of the Christ mind.

> **Christ also did not take upon himself**
> **the glory of becoming a high priest.**
> **But God said to him, You are my Son;**
> **today I have become your Father.**
> **Hebrews 5:5**

Because his bloodline came from the line of King David, Jesus was the heir to the throne of the Kingdom of Israel. So, when he was just a toddler, his parents took him to Alexandria, in Egypt, out of the fear of persecution by the reigning King Herod. There, they stayed with two masters who taught them about what was to become of their son. The holy family lived in Egypt until the death of King Herod, and then returned to their home in Nazareth.

Trade routes with the Far East were opening up around this time and commerce between Egypt and India was achieved by way of Nazareth. Largely gentile in population, it was a caravan way station and a crossroads of travel.

When Jesus was thirteen years of age, a royal prince of India led him by caravan into the desert toward the Earth's kundalini energy. When he arrived in India a year later, Jesus was accepted as a pupil in the temple

The Fall

Jagannath. With the intention of perfecting himself and learning the laws that had been written by Gautama, the Buddha, he set about gaining wisdom through the Vedas.

Over time, the Brahmic priests tried to drive Jesus out of India because he didn't totally agree with their ways. As a result, he fled to a temple in Lassa, Tibet, where he was given access to sacred manuscripts that were rich in ancient lore. When he finished his studies in the temple schools, he journeyed to the Ladak city of Leh to live and study in their monastery.

At the age of twenty-five, Jesus began the journey west and boarded a ship for Greece to study with the masters there. Then, he traveled to the holy temple of Heliopolis in Egypt, where he met with the seven great sages and took the vow of the secret brotherhood.

Because of the seven initiations that must be completed in order to attain the mind of Christ, the symbols of the perfect man are the circle and the number seven. So it was by the symbol of a seven enclosed within a circle that Jesus became known to the great sages. And, when he had passed the first initiation of the brotherhood, he received his first degree - that of Sincerity. When he passed the tests of Justice, Faith, Philanthrophy, Heroism and Divine Love, he also received those degrees.

With six degrees, he entered the senior course of study, which dealt with the secrets of Egypt, the mysteries

The Fall

of life, death and the worlds beyond the Sun. When he had passed the seventh and final initiation, Jesus received his seventh degree - that of Christ.

While Jesus lived on the Earth, his awareness of his Spirit remained intact. And, although he wrestled with his sub-conscious, he learned how to place himself into Timeless Space and command it. When his Spirit prevailed, his ministry in Israel began.

> **And the child grew and became strong in Spirit; and he lived in the desert until he appeared publicly to Israel.**
> **Luke 1:80**

Because Jesus was able to control the laws that govern this material plane, he was a threat to the Jewish ruling order of the time. Subsequently, three years into his ministry in Israel, they conspired to have him crucified by the Roman army.

> **Unless I go away, the Counselor will not come to you; but if I go, I will send him to you...**
> **John 16:7**

The story of Jesus' adult life in Israel is fairly common knowledge. But, what isn't commonly understood is that he was able to balance the basic chemical elements of his physical body. His DNA was transformed into a thirty-three double-strand DNA matrix, which completely illuminated his body into a glorified body of Light - a powerful vehicle of ascension.

The Fall

Simply by living, dying, and then resurrecting his body, Jesus placed into the global akashic field all of the secrets he knew and learned as a mortal man who attained Christ consciousness. This encoded them in our DNA.

> **He will bring glory to me**
> **by taking from what is mine**
> **and making it known to you.**
> **The secret of the kingdom of God**
> **has been given to you.**
> John 16:25 and Mark 4:11

After his resurrection, Jesus materialized before the seven sages and said to them, "My human life was wholly given to bring my will to tune with the deific will. With this done, my Earth tasks all were done. You know that all my life was one great drama for the sons of men - a pattern for the sons of men. I lived to show the possibilities of Man. What I have done all men can do and what I am all men shall be."

> **He appeared to more than five hundred**
> **of the brothers at the same time,**
> **most of whom are still living,**
> **though some have Fallen Asleep.**
> I Corinthians 15:5-6

He then stood on the Mount of Olives and, raising his hands, he professed, "The benedictions of the Holy Ones, of the almighty God and of the Holy breath, of Christ - the love of God made manifest, will rest upon you all the way 'till you shall rise and sit with me upon the throne of power."

Then he ascended to God...

The Fall

Afterword

Precisely one-hundred years before the year 2012, a book called *The Kybalion* was published anonymously under the pseudonym of The Three Initiates. This book is a study of the Hermetic Philosophy of ancient Egypt and Greece - the essence of the teachings of Hermes Trismegistus and the seven divine laws. Within this book, is written the following:

> **The Earth is a mere grain of dust in the Universe. There are millions upon millions of such worlds, of which some are far greater than our own. And there are millions of universes within the infinite divine mind.**
>
> **Even in our own solar system, there are regions and planes of life far higher than ours, with attributes greater than we have ever dreamed. Yet, these beings were once ourselves.**
>
> **The Three Initiates**

In this age, it is God's will for us to reunite with Him. So we are seeking to raise our frequency and remember our true nature. The Inbreath of God has begun. There are 352 initiations we must pass to completely merge with God. But we will be as we were before and still greater - for such is the Destiny of Man.

Metanoia
Change your mind

About the Author

The Atlantean energy is one of great mental power combined with a distinctive pride. Thousands of years ago, Vicky Anderson used telepathic powers to program Crystals, and to access and retrieve records from a vast library of information on the great continent called Atlantis.

Today, Vicky is a researcher and historian who has previously written eight historical guides to the West Coast of Canada. She currently lives on Vancouver Island, British Columbia, and is self-employed as an energy worker at the Hidden Lighthouse Wellness Center - the only clinic on all of the island to offer the type of Energy Medicine that is described in this book.

Vicky is bridging Christianity and Eastern Mysticism with Western Science to provide a crystal clear picture of the history of man and what is really happening to mankind today. She maintains an eZine of current and relevant information at the website listed below.

The Hidden Lighthouse eZine
www.hiddenlighthouse.com/eZine

The Hidden Lighthouse Wellness Center
Victoria, BC
Canada
250-744-6442
www.hiddenlighthouse.com

Suggested Reading

The Sermon on the Mount According to Vedanta, Swami Prabhavananda, Vedanta Press, 1991

The Sermon on the Mount: The Key to Success in Life, Emmet Fox, HarperOne, 1989

The Perfection of Yoga, A. C. Bhaktivedanta Swami Prabhupada, Bhaktivedanta Book Trust, 1974

The Unknown Life of Jesus: The Original Text of Nicolas Notovitch's 1887 Discovery, Nicolas Notovitch, translated by J. H. Connelly, and L. Landsberg, Quill Driver Books, 2004

Flower Essences and Vibrational Healing, Gurudas, Cassandra Press, 1986

The Gnostic Gospels, Elaine Pagels, Vintage Books, 1989

Mending the Past and Healing the Future with Soul Retrieval, Alberto Villoldo, Hay House, 2006

Spirit Communication: The Soul's Path, Kevin Ryerson and Stephanie Harolde, Bantam, 1991

The Future Healer: Spirit Communication on Healing, Ronald Henry, iUniverse, Inc., 2007

The Divine Matrix, Gregg Braden, Hay House, 2008

Awakening to Zero Point: The Collective Initiation, Gregg Braden, Sacred Spaces Ancient Wisdom 1997

The Kybalion, Three Initiates, Tarcher; 1st Jeremy P. Tarcher/Penguin Ed edition, 2008

Jesus and Buddha, Marcus Borg, Ulysses Press, 2005

Healing Codes for the Biological Apocalypse, Dr. Len Horowitz, Healthy World Distribution, 1999

Energy Medicine: The Scientific Basis, James L. Oschman, Churchill Livingstone, 2000

The Case for Reincarnation, Joe Fisher, Somerville House Publishing, 1998

Jesus and the Essenes, Dolores Cannon , Ozark Mountain Publishing Inc., 1999

Misquoting Jesus: The Story Behind Who Changed the Bible and Why, Bart D. Ehrman, HarperOne, 2007

The Aquarian Gospel of Jesus the Christ, Levi H. Dowling, Tarcher, 2009

Ask Your Angels, Alma Daniel, Timothy Wyllie and Andrew Ramer, Ballantine Books, 1992

Divine Guidance, Doreen Virtue, St. Martin's Griffin, 1998

Pyramid Power, Max Toth and Greg Nielsen, Destiny Books, 1985

The Secret Life of Plants, Peter Tompkins and Christopher Bird, Harper Paperbacks, 1989

The Biology of Belief: Unleashing the Power of Consciousness, Matter and Miracles, Bruce H. Lipton, Ph.D., Hay House, 2008

Suggested Viewing

Crossing the Event Horizon, Nassim Haramein, 2008

The Gospel of John, Buena Vista Home Entertainment/Disney, 2003

Healing the Luminous Body - The Way of the Shaman, Sacred Mysteries Productions, 2004

ORBS: Clues to a More Exciting Universe, Edessa Code LLC

How Jesus Became a Christ: Deep Deceptions Volume 2, Edessa Code LLC, 2006

The Celestine Prophecy, Sony Pictures, 2006

NOVA: The Elegant Universe, WGBH Boston, 2004

The Matrix, Warner Home Video, 1999

The Cross of Thoth, Reality Ent., 2007

Quantum Astrology, Sacred Mysteries Productions, 2005

The Great Year, The Yuga Project, 2003

Star Dreams, A Feature Documentary Exploring the Mystery of the Crop Circles, Genesis Communications, 2007

Suggested Visiting

Krishna.com
www.krishna.com

The Shift of the Ages
www.shiftingages.com

The Quantum Activist
www.quantumactivist.com

The Spirit of Ma'at
www.spiritofmaat.com

Institute for Cultural Awareness
www.ica8.org

The Four Winds Society
www.thefourwinds.com

Music From God
www.musicfromgod.com

Bruce H. Lipton, Ph.D
www.brucelipton.com

Lightning Path™
www.thelightningpath.com

Eckhart Tolle
www.eckharttolle.com

Global Coherence Initiative
www.glcoherence.org

The Gnostic Society
www.gnosis.org

Internet Sacred Text Archive
www.sacred-texts.com

The Lunar Planner
www.lunarplanner.com

Free Conscious Media Network
www.consciousmedianetwork.com

SPIRITube
www.spiritube.com

New Millennium Essences
www.nmessences.com

Body Mind Connection
www.bodymindconnection.ca

Skylight Paths
www.skylightpaths.com

Vedanta Press
www.vedanta.com

Namaste Publishing
www.namastepublishing.com

Best Words Publishing
www.beyondword.com

HADO
www.hadousa.com

Cymatics
www.cymaticsource.com

The Lost Books
www.thelostbooks.com

Ra Music
www.ramusic.com

AngelTherapy.Com
www.angeltherapy.com

Academy of Sacred Geometry
www.academysacredgeometry.com

Jain MatheMagics
www.jainmathemagics.com

I AM University
www.iamuniversity.org/iamu

The String Theory Website
www.superstringtheory.com

DeanRadin.com
www.deanradin.com

BioGeometry
www.biogeometry.com

Timewave One Calculator
www.timewave2012.com

Global Coherence Initiative
www.glcoherence.org

The Resonance Project
www.theresonanceproject.org

The Intention Experiment
www.intentionexperiment.com

kundalini Research Foundation Ltd.
www.kundaliniresearch.org

The Summit Lighthouse
www.tsl.org

Quantum K
www.quantumk.co.uk

Free Sahaja Meditation Classes
www.freemeditation.ca/classes

Free Sahaja Meditation Online
www.onlinemeditation.ca

Trust Your Vibes
www.trustyourvibes.com

Amit Goswami
www.amitgoswami.org

Mindbridge-LOA.com
www.mindbridge-loa.org

Time Machine 1212
www.timemachine1212.com

Bibliography

[1] *The Four Insights: Wisdom, Power, and Grace of the Earthkeepers*, Alberto Villoldo, Hay House, 2007

[2] *Legend of the Rainbow Warriors*, Steven McFadden, Harlem Writers Guild Press, 2005

[3] *The Biology of Belief: Unleashing the Power of Consciousness, Matter and Miracles*, Bruce H. Lipton, Ph.D., Hay House, 2008

[4] *The Body Electric: Electomagnetism and the Foundation of Life*, Robert O. Becker and Gary Seldon, Harper Paperbacks, 1998

[5] *The Relation of Vaccine Therapy to Homeopathy*, Edward Bach, British Homeopathy Journal, 1920

[6] *The Role of the Bowel Flora in Chronic Disease*, John Patterson, British Homeopathic Journal, 1949

[7] *Flower Essences and Vibrational Healing*, Gurudas, Casandra Press, 1989

[8] The Hidden Energy Science of Sacred Geometry, Robert J. Gilbert

[9] *Pyramid Power*, Max Toth and Greg Nielsen, Destiny Books, 1985

[10] RA Research Society

[11] *The Baptist Revelation*, Gary Osborn, 2006

[12] *The God Hypothesis: Discovering Design in Our Just Right Goldilocks Universe*, Michael Anthony Corey, Rowman & Littlefield Publishers, 2007

[13] RA Research Society

[14] *Healing Codes for the Biological Apocalypse*, Dr. Len Horowitz, Healthy World Distribution, 1999

[15] *Music From God,* www.musicfromgod.com

[16] *Approaching Timewave Zero*, Terence McKenna

[17] Guatemala, Cradle of the Maya Civilization website

[18] *What is the Origin of Spin?*, Nassim Haramein

[19] *Awakening to Zero Point: The Collective Initiation*, Gregg Braden, Sacred Spaces Ancient Wisdom 1997

[20] *In Resonance*, Jasmuheen, KOHA Publishing, 1999

[21] *Buddha and Christ: Nativity Stories and Indian Traditions*, Zacharias P. Thundy, Brill Academic Publishers, 1992

[22] *Buddhist and Christian Gospels: Being Gospel Parallels from Pali Texts*, Albert J. Edmunds, Kessinger Publishing, LLC , 2007

[23] *Suns of God: Krishna, Buddha and Christ Unveiled*, Acharya S, Adventures Unlimited Press, 2004

[24] *Silicon conducts an electrical surprise,* Royal Society of Chemistry, February, 2006

[25] *Oppenheimer and the Manhattan Project*, Cynthia C. Kelly, World Scientific Publishing, 2006

[26] Nature Journal, Cornell, et al, 1997

[27] Lifestream Associates, LLC

[28] Vogel Crystals, Curtis Lang

[29] *The Biological Chip in Our Cells: Revolutionary Results of Modern Genetics*, Grazyna Fosar and Franz Bludorf

[30] *The Biology of Belief: An Interview with Dr. Bruce Lipton*, Lotus Guide: May/ June 2005

[31] *The DNA PHANTOM EFFECT: Direct Measurement of A New Field in the Vacuum Substructure*, Dr. Vladimir Poponin

[32] New Crystal in the Pineal Gland: Characterization and Potential Role in Electro-mechano-Transduction, Dr. Sidney B. Lang, Dr. Rene de Seze and Dr. Simon Baconnier

[33] New Crystal in the Pineal Gland: Characterization and Potential Role in Electro-mechano-Transduction, Dr. Sidney B. Lang, Dr. Rene de Seze and Dr. Simon Baconnier

[34] *The Bridge to Infinity*, Bruce L. Cathie, Adventures Unlimited Press, 1997

[35] Website of Dr. Jill Bolte Taylor

[36] *Shri Mataji Nirmala Devi,* Sahaja Yoga Canada

[37] *GAIA - A New Look at Life on Earth*, James Lovelock, Oxford University Press, Oxford, 1979

[38] CNN.com/SPACE, March 21, 2002

[39] Barbara Brennan School of Healing website.

[40] *Mending the Past and Healing the Future with Soul Retrieval*, Alberto Villoldo, Hay House, 2006 and *New York Open Center*, Interview with Alberto Villoldo

[41] *CIA-Initiated Remote Viewing At Stanford Research Institute*, H. E. Puthoff, Ph.D.

[42] *The Energetic Vacuum: Implications For Energy Research*, H.E. Puthoff, PhD

[43] *The Ego and the Id*, Sigmund Freud, The Hogarth Press Ltd. London, 1949

[44] *Can Science And Spirituality Be Reconciled?*, Amit Goswami, Science Within Consciousness, Volume 1, No 2; 1996

[45] Extended Analysis: September 11, 2001 in Context, Global Consciousness Project, Princeton University

[46] *Two Thousand years of Coptic Christianity*, Otto F.A. Meinardus

[47] *The Jewish War*, Flavius Josephus, Penguin Classics, 1984

[48] *The Gnostic Gospels*, Elaine Pagels, Vintage Books, 1989

[49] The Friedberg Genizah Project website

[50] *The Gospel of Thomas: The Hidden Sayings of Jesus*, Marvin Meyer, HarperOne; 2nd edition, 1992

[51] *The Gnostic Gospels*, Elaine Pagels, Vintage Books, 1989

[52] *Mysteries of the Dead Sea Scrolls*, New Liberty Videos, 2006

[53] *English Bible History*, John L. Jeffcoat III with special thanks to Dr. Craig H. Lampe, International Director of the World Bible Society, www.greatsite.com

[54] *The Lost Books of the Bible: The Real Apocrypha*, Patrick Cooke, Oracle Research Publishing, 2005

[55] Quantum Resonance website

[56] *The Four Insights: Wisdom, Power, and Grace of the Earthkeepers*, Alberto Villoldo, Hay House, 2007

[57] *Shadow of the Third Century: A Revaluation of Christianity*, Alvin Boyd Kuhn, Academy Press, 1949, and Augnet website

[58] *How Jesus Became a Christ: The Hidden Years. Vol. 2 of Deep Deceptions*, Edessa Code LLC, 2006

www.ingramcontent.com/pod-product-compliance
Lightning Source LLC
Chambersburg PA
CBHW070752100426
42742CB00012B/2109